George Stibitz

Outlines of the Bible..

George Stibitz
Outlines of the Bible..
ISBN/EAN: 9783337171735

Printed in Europe, USA, Canada, Australia, Japan

Cover: Foto ©Lupo / pixelio.de

More available books at **www.hansebooks.com**

OUTLINES

OF

THE BIBLE:

THE BIBLICAL (INCLUDING THE APOCRYPHAL) BOOKS ANALYZED
AND CHRONOLOGICALLY ARRANGED UNDER THE
OUTLINES OF BIBLICAL HISTORY,

WITH A

CLASSIFIED LIST OF HELPS TO BIBLE STUDY.

BY

GEORGE STIBITZ, Ph. D. (Yale),

PROFESSOR OF HEBREW AND OLD TESTAMENT THEOLOGY, AND INSTRUCTOR OF THE
ENGLISH BIBLE IN URSINUS COLLEGE, COLLEGEVILLE, PA.

Ye shall know the truth, and the truth shall make you free.—John 8: 32.

NORRISTOWN, PA.:
HERALD PRINTING AND BINDING ROOMS.
1892.

Entered, according to Act of Congress, in the year 1892, by

GEORGE STIBITZ, Ph. D.,

In the Office of the Librarian of Congress at Washington.

PREFACE.

These outlines of the Bible are not supposed to be matured. Much time and labor might well have been spent on them to give them anything like a finish. But desiring to use the valuable time of teacher and student to better advantage than that of dictating and writing, I had them printed as they now are. The very fact, however, that they are by no means in all cases final, gives them a greater educational value for the student, who is expected not to abide by them but to verify or improve them.

The analysis of the different books of the Bible is, of course, not original with me. The material, more or less as it is here, has been gathered from various sources, and modified and arranged to suit the present purpose.

These outlines are intended to aid in acquiring a knowledge of the Bible nearly in the order in which it is commonly supposed to have been written, the poetic, prophetic and epistolary portions being inserted where they chronologically belong; and to aid in gaining such an acquaintance with the Bible as to enable one to pass the books before his mind, and tell their contents by parts and sections if not by chapters. To this end the parts and sections of the books have been gathered together under the historical periods in the fore part of the book, and in the body of the work the chapters have been left as unbroken as possible. The "Synopsis," both "by Stages and Epochs" and "by Periods," should be well mastered as the study of the Bible progresses.

The Apocrypha have been added because they contain much

valuable material and are not regarded as canonic. A knowledge of them is important for the understanding of the New Testament Judaism.

The full plan of these outlines, which I hope some time to complete, is to include a more detailed work on the subdivisions of the chapters, outlines and helps on important topics under each period, and summaries of Biblical information on the men, places, etc., which have come up in the course of the outlines.

It was thought best not to bring questions of modern criticism into these outlines, but rather to put all the efforts on the more important work of acquiring a knowledge of the Bible.

SYNOPSIS OF BIBLICAL HISTORY.

BY STAGES AND EPOCHS.

First Stage: The Theocracy, or direct rule of God.
Theologically, Mosaism.
Creation, 4004 —Anointing of Saul, 1095.
Epoch I. The Primitive World.
  Creation, 4004.—Call of Abraham, 1921.
Epoch II. The History of the Patriarchs.
  Call of Abraham, 1921.—Birth of Moses, 1571.
Epoch III. The Theocratic Nation.
  Birth of Moses, 1571.—Anointing of Saul, 1095.

Second Stage: The Monarchy, or rule of Kings.
Theologically, Prophetism and Wisdom.
Anointing of Saul, 1095.—Captivity of Judah, 587.
Epoch I. The Undivided Monarchy.
  Anointing of Saul, 1095.—Revolt of Israel, 975.
Epoch II. The Divided Monarchy.
  Revolt of Israel, 975.—Fall of Samaria, 721.
Epoch III. Judah Alone.
  Fall of Samaria, 721.—Captivity of Judah, 587.

Third Stage: The Hierocracy, or rule of Priests.
Theologically, Judaism.
Captivity of Judah, 587.—End of Jewish State, A. D. 70.
Epoch I. Closing Epoch of O. T. History.
  Captivity of Judah, 587.—End of Old Testament, 400.
Epoch II. Intertestamentary History.
  End of Old Testament, 400.—Birth of Christ, B. C. 4.
Epoch III. New Testament History.
  Birth of Christ, B. C. 4.—End of Jewish State, A. D. 70.

BY PERIODS.

4004.	1.	Age of Adam	Gen.	1–5.
2348.	2.	Age of Noah	"	6–11.
1921.	3.	Age of Abraham	"	12–25 : 18.
1857.	4.	Age of Isaac and Jacob	"	25 : 19–36.
	5.	Age of Joseph	"	37–50.
1745.		a) History of Joseph		37–45.
1706.		b) Israel in Bondage		46–50.

THE BOOK OF JOB.

Part I.	The Prologue	1–2.
Part II.	The Discussion	3–31.
§1.	First Circle of Speeches	4–14.
§2.	Second Circle of Speeches	15–21.
§3.	Third Circle of Speeches	22–31.
Part III.	The Speeches of Elihu	32–37.
Part IV.	Jehovah's Answer to Job	38–42 : 6.
Part V.	The Epilogue	42 : 7–17.

1571. 6. Age of Moses. Ex., Lev., Num. and Deut.

1491. EXODUS: DELIVERANCE AND ESTABLISHMENT OF ISRAEL.

Part I.	Deliverance from Egypt	1–18.
§1.	Preparation for deliverance	1–6.
§2.	Miraculous deliverance	7–14.
§3.	Israel's march from Red Sea to Sinai	15–18.
Part II.	God's Covenant with Israel	19–40.
§1.	The laws of the Covenant	19–24.
§2.	Divine directions for the Tabernacle	25–31.
§3.	Covenant broken and renewed	32–34.
§4.	Construction of the Tabernacle	35–40.

LEVITICUS, CEREMONIAL LAWS.

Part I.	Sacrificial Laws	1–7.
Part II.	Inauguration of Priesthood	8–10.
Part III.	Purification Laws. Atonement	11–16.
Part IV.	Laws for Israel as a holy people	17–27.

NUMBERS, ISRAEL'S LIFE IN THE WILDERNESS.

Part I.	Preparation for departure from Sinai	1–9.
Part II.	Israel's journeys—Sinai to Moab	10–21.
§1.	Journey—Sinai to Kadesh Barnea	10–14.
§2.	Wanderings in the Wilderness	15–19.
§3.	Journey—Kadesh Barnea to Moab	20–21.
Part III.	Events and laws at Moab	22–36.

DEUTERONOMY, FAREWELL ADDRESS OF MOSES.

Part I.	The First Address	1–4.
§1.	Review of Israel's History	1–3.
§2.	Exhortation to serve God	4.
Part II.	The Second Address	5–26.
§1.	On the First and Second Commandments	5–11.
§2.	On particular laws	12–26.
Part III.	The Third Address	27–30.
Part IV.	Close of his life and works	31–34.

1451. 7. Age of Joshua.

BOOK OF JOSHUA.

Part I.	Deeds of war—Conquest of Canaan	1–12.
§1.	Crossing the Jordan	1–5.
§2.	Conquest of the South	6–10.
§3.	Conquest of the North	11–12.
Part II.	Works of peace—Possession of Canaan	13–24.
§1.	Division of the Land	13–19.
§2.	Refuge and Levitical Cities	20–21.
§3.	Last days of Joshua	22–24.

1400. 8. Age of the Judges.

BOOK OF THE JUDGES.

PART I.	Historical narrative	1-16.
§1.	From Joshua to Shamgar	1-3.
§2.	Deborah and Barak	4-5.
§3.	Gideon and his family	6-9.
§4.	Jephthah of Gilead	10-12.
§5.	Samson's life and works	13-16.
PART II.	Appendixes—State of society	17-21. Ruth.
§1.	Idolatry of Dan	17-18.
§2.	Benjamin's sin and punishment	19-21.
§3.	"Light amid the encircling gloom"	Ruth 1-4.

I SAMUEL.

1115.	9.	Age of Samuel, the Reformer	1-7.
1095.	10.	Reign of Saul, 40 years	8-31.
		§1. Saul appointed king	8-10.
		§2. Saul's reign till his rejection	11-15.
		§3. Decline of Saul and rise of David	16-31.
		a) David's private life	16-17.
		b) David's court life	18-20.
		c) David's outlaw life	21-31.
1055.	11.	Reign of David	

II SAMUEL.

		II Sam.	I Chron.
PART I.	David's prosperous reign	1-10.	
§1.	David's reign over Judah alone	1-4.	
§2.	Rise of David's power	5-10.	11-19.
PART II.	David's calamitous reign	11-24.	
§1.	David's sin and repentance	11-12.	
§2.	David's punishment	13-20.	
§3.	Supplement to David's reign	21-24.	20-29.

THE PSALTER, O. T. CHURCH HYMNAL.

BOOK I.	Davidic Psalms	1-41.
BOOK II.	Davidic and Levitic Psalms	42-72.
BOOK III.	Psalms of various authorship	73-89.
BOOK IV.	Mostly anonymous Psalms	90-106.
BOOK V.	Davidic and Pilgrimage Psalms	107-150.

1015. 12. Reign of Solomon. I Kings, 1-11. II Chron., 1-9.

BOOK OF PROVERBS.

PART I.	Introduction—Discourse on wisdom	1-9.
PART II.	First collection of Solomonic Proverbs	10-22 : 16.
PART III.	Appendixes to first collection	22 : 17-24.
§1.	Words of Wise Men	22 : 17-24 : 22.
§2.	Words of Wise Men	24 : 23-34.
PART IV.	Second collection of Solomonic Proverbs	25-29.
PART V.	Appendixes to second collection	30-31.
§1.	Words of Agur	30.
§2.	Words of King Lemuel	31 : 1-9.
§3.	Acrostic hymn—The virtuous woman	31 : 10-31.

SONG OF SOLOMON.

PART I.	First meeting of the lovers	1-2 : 7.
PART II.	Their mutual longing and seeking	2 : 8-3 : 5.
PART III.	The wedding in the royal city	3 : 6-5 : 1.
PART IV.	Love's new seeking and longing	5 : 2-8 : 4.
PART V.	The sealing and meaning of the covenant	8 : 5-14.

KOHELETH OR ECCLESIASTES.

PART I.	The speaker introduced	1 : 1–11.
PART II.	Koheleth retraces his experience	1 : 12–3 : 22.
PART III.	Wrongs and miseries	4.
PART IV.	Consideration of topics	5 : 1–6 : 12.
PART V.	Lessons from hope, freedom, etc.	7.
PART VI.	Disproportion in the world	8 : 1–9 : 10.
PART VII.	Disproportion in life	9 : 11–10 : 20.
PART VIII.	Closing reflection	11 : 1–12 : 7.
PART IX.	Epilogue	12 : 8–14.

JUDAH.   ISRAEL.

975. **13.** Period of Division. I Kings, 12–II Kings, 8. II Chron., 10–21.

Division to accession of Jehu.

JUDAH	ISRAEL
Reign of Rehoboam.	House of Jeroboam.
Reign of Asa.	House of Baasha.
Reign of Jehoshaphat.	House of Omri.
	Elijah, the Prophet.

884. **14.** Syrian Period. II Kings, 9–13 : 9. II Chron., 21–24.

Accession of Jehu to that of Amaziah and Joash.

JUDAH	ISRAEL
Reign of Athaliah.	Reign of Jehu.
Reign of Jehoash.	Reign of Jehoahaz.
Obadiah : Against Edom.	

840. **15.** Restoration of Israel. II Kings, 13 : 10–15 : 17. II Chron., 25, 26.

Accession of Amaziah and Joash to end of Jeroboam II.

JUDAH	ISRAEL
Reign of Amaziah.	Reign of Jehoash.
Reign of Uzziah.	Reign of Jeroboam II.
Joel: Call to repentance.	JONAH : God's saving love.
PART I. Judgment. Repentance, 1–2 : 17.	
PART II. Promises, 2 : 18–4.	

780. **16.** Fall of Israel. II Kings, 15 : 18–17. II Chron., 27, 28.

End of Jeroboam II to Fall of Samaria.

JUDAH	ISRAEL
Reign of Jotham.	Reign of Menahem.
Reign of Ahaz.	Reign of Pekah.
MICAH :	Reign of Hoshea.
PART I. Doom and hope of Israel, 1–5.	AMOS : ISRAEL'S RUIN.
PART II. God's lawsuit, 6–7.	PART I. Judgment, 1–2.
	PART II. Sermons, 3–6.
ISAIAH :	PART III. Visions, 7–9 : 10.
PART I. 1–39.	PART IV. Restoration, 9 : 11–15.
§ 1. Judah reproved, 1–6.	HOSEA :
§ 2. Emanuel Book, 7–12.	GOD'S FAITHFULNESS.
	PART I. Symbolic prophecy, 1–3.
	PART II. Sermons, 4–14.

721.	17.	Age of Hezekiah. II Kings, 18–20. II Chron. 29–32.		
		(Isa.) § 3. Oracles against the nations		13–23.
		§ 4. Prophecies—End of the world		24–27.
		§ 5. Prophecies concerning Zion		28–35.
		§ 6. Appendix, concerning future		36–39.

NAHUM: PROPHECY AGAINST NINEVEH, 1–3.

698. 18. Fall of Jerusalem. II Kings, 21–25. II Chron. 33–36. *Manasseh to Zedekiah.*

HABAKKUK: AGAINST THE WORLD POWERS, 1–3.

ZEPHENIAH: DAY OF WRATH AND PROMISE, 1–3.

JEREMIAH.

PART I.	Prophecy and history relating to Judah	1–45.
§ 1.	Addresses in time of Josiah	1–10.
§ 2.	Addresses in time of Jehoikim and Jehoiakin	11–20.
§ 3.	Addresses in time of Zedekiah	21–24,
§ 4.	Special prophecies of the Overthrow	25–29.
§ 5.	Book of Comfort	30–33.
§ 6.	Utterances in time of Jehoikim and Zedekiah	34–39.
§ 7.	Jeremiah's work after fall of Jerusalem	40–45.
PART II.	Prophecies against the nations	46–51.
	LAMENTATIONS OVER JERUSALEM	1–5.

587. 19. Babylonian Captivity.

EZEKIEL.

PART I.	Before the Siege: Judgment	1–24.
§ 1.	Ezekiel's call and first work	1–7.
§ 2.	Concerning expulsion, 6th year	8–19.
§ 3.	Against idolatry, 7th year	20–24.
PART II.	During the Siege: Transition	25–32.
PART III.	After the Siege: Mercy	33–48.
§ 1.	Divine promises	33–39.
§ 2.	The New Jerusalem	40–48.

HISTORY OF SUSANNA. (Apoch.)

DANIEL.

PART I.	History of Daniel's time	1–6.
PART II.	Visions of Daniel	7–12.
	Bel and the Dragon. (Apoch.)	

ISAIAH. (Written in time of Hezekiah.)

PART II.	Comfort to the Exiles	40–66.
§ 1.	God's preparation for Israel's salvation	40–48.
§ 2.	Exaltation of the Servant and Zion	49–57.
§ 3.	Completion of salvation	58–66.

HISTORY OF TOBIT. (Apoch.)

HISTORY OF JUDITH. (Apoch.)

536. 20. Persian Period. Ezra, Nehemiah.

EZRA. RETURN OF CAPTIVITY.

PART I.	First return of captives	1–6.
PART II.	Ezra and his work	7–10.

HAGGAI: Exhortation to build temple, 1-2.

ZECHARIAH.

Part I.	Visions	1-6.
Part II.	Decisions about fast-days	7-8.
Part III.	Israel's security and triumph	9-11.
Part IV.	Israel's final victory	12-14.

ESTHER.

NEHEMIAH.

Part I.	Restoration of Jerusalem	1-7.
Part II.	Ezra's solemn service	8 10.
Part III.	Various lists and accounts	11-13.

I ESRDRAS, 1-9.

II ESRDRAS, 1-16.

MALACHI: Rebuke of priests and people, 1-4.

333. 21. Grecian Period.

ECCLESIASTICUS (cir. 300).

168. 22. Jewish Independence.
to
63. I MACCABEES: Jewish war of independence.

Part I.	History of Mattathias	1-2.
Part II.	History of Judas	3-9 : 22.
Part III.	History of Jonathan	9 : 23-12.
Part IV.	History of Simon	13-16.

II MACCABEES: History of Judas.

Part I.	Two letters to Egyptian Jews	1-2.
Part II.	Internal and external troubles	3-10 : 9.
Part III.	Jewish victories	10 : 10-15.

BARUCH.

WISDOM OF SOLOMON.

Part I.	Wisdom, moral and intellectual	1-9.
§1.	Wisdom the source of immortality	1-5.
§2.	Wisdom the guide of life	6-9.
Part II.	Wisdom in history	10-19.
§1.	Wisdom a power to save and chastise	10-12.
§2.	Growth of idolatry against wisdom	13-14.
§3.	True worship over against idolatry	15-19.

B. C. 4. 23. The Life of Christ.
§1. The Preparation. 30 years.
Matthew 1-2. Mark —. Luke 1-2. John 1 : 1-18.
§2. The Inauguration. 15 months.
Matthew 3-4 : 12. Mark 1 : 1-14. Luke 3-4 : 15. John 1 : 19-4.
§3. The Early Galilean Ministry. 4 months.
Matthew 4 : 13-7. Mark 1 : 15-3 : 19. Luke 4 : 16-6. John 5.
§4. The Later Galilean Ministry. 10 months.
Matthew 8-14. Mark 3 : 19-6. Luke 7-9 : 17. John 6.
§5. The Retirement. 6 months.
Matthew 15-18. Mark 7-9. Luke 9 : 18-50. John —.
§6. The Judean Ministry. 3 months.
Matthew —. Mark —. Luke 9 : 51-13 : 21. John 7-10.

§7. The Perean Ministry. 4 months.
Matthew 19–20. Mark 10. Luke 13 : 22–19 : 28.   John 11–12 : 11.
§8. The Passion Week.
Matthew 21–27. Mark 11–15.   Luke 19 : 29–23.   John 12–19.
§9. The Resurrection. 40 days.
Matthew 28. Mark 16. Luke 24. John 20.

24. The Petrine Period. Jewish Christianity. Acts 1–12.
 §1. The founding of the church . . . .   1–2.
 §2. The church in Jerusalem . . . .   3–7.
 §3. The Church in Judea, Samaria and Antioch . . .   8–12.
 §4. Epistles.

  JUDE : DEFENCE OF THE FAITH.

  JAMES : CHRISTIAN PRACTICE, 1–5.

  I PETER : STAND FAST IN THE FAITH.
 PART I. Blessings of Christians . . . .   1–2 : 10.
 PART II. Duties of Christians . . . .   2 : 11–5.

  II PETER : KNOWLEDGE NOT FABLES AS SCOFFERS SAY, 1–3.

  HEBREWS : SUPERIORITY OF THE NEW DISPENSATION.
 PART I. Christ's superiority over all mediators . . . . .   1–4.
 PART II. High Priesthood of Christ . . . .   5–7.
 PART III. Christ's new and better covenant . . . . . .   8–10.
 PART IV. Consequent practical lessons . . . .   11–13.

25. Pauline Period. Gentile Christianity. Acts 13–28.
 §1. First Missionary Journey . . . .   Acts 13–14.
 §2. Second Missionary Journey . . . . Acts 15–18 : 22.
 §3. First group of Epistles : On eschatology.

  I THESS : CONSOLATION IN VIEW OF SECOND ADVENT.
 PART I. Review of his relation to them . . . .   1–3.
 PART II. Exhortation and Consolation . . . .   4–5.

  II THESS : PATIENT WAITING FOR THE DAY OF THE LORD.
 §4. Third Missionary Journey . . . . Acts 18 : 23–21 : 16
 §5. Second group of Epistles : Judaic controversy.

  I CORINTHIANS : ON MORALITY AND DISCIPLINE.
 PART I. The sin of partisan spirit . . . .   1–4.
 PART II. Disorders in the Corinthian Church . . . . . .   5–6.
 PART III. Answers to their questions . . . .   7–16.

  II CORINTHIANS : PAUL'S DEFENCE OF HIS OFFICE.
 PART I. His apostolic character and conduct . . . . . .   1–7.
 PART II. Collections for the poor . . . .   8–9.
 PART III. Direct personal self defence . . . .   10–13.

  GALATIANS : CHRISTIAN LIBERTY.
 PART I. Personal : Vindication of his apostleship . . . .   1–2.
 PART II. Doctrinal : Freedom from the Law . . . . . .   3–4.
 PART III. Practical exhortations . . . .   5–6.

  ROMANS : SALVATION BY FAITH.
 PART I. Christ our righteousness . . . .   1–5.
  §1. Universal need of justification . . . .   1 : 18–3 : 20.
  §2. How salvation is attained . . . .   3 : 21–c. 5.
 PART II. Christ our sanctification . . . .   6–8.

PART III. The temporary rejection of the Jews . . . . .   9–11.
PART IV. Exhortation and instruction . . . .   12–16.
§5. Paul's imprisonment . . . . Acts 21 : 17–28.
§6. Third group of Epistles: Personal and Christological.

PHILIPPIANS: PAUL'S LOVE TO THE PHILIPPIANS, 1–4.

COLOSSIANS: CHRIST IS ALL IN ALL, 1–4.

PHILEMON: PAUL'S INTERCESSION FOR ONESIMUS.

EPHESIANS: THE GLORY OF OUR SALVATION.
PART I. Glory of the Church of Christ . . . .   1–3.
PART II. Walk worthy of your calling . . . .   4–6.
§6. Fourth group of Epistles: Pastoral.

I TIMOTHY: PAUL'S CHARGE TO TIMOTHY, 1–6.

TITUS: PAUL'S INSTRUCTIONS TO TITUS, 1–3.

II TIMOTHY: PAUL'S LAST LETTER, 1–4.

26. Johannean Period: Spiritual Christianity.

THE GOSPEL OF JOHN: BELIEVE IN CHRIST AND LIVE.
PART I. Development of faith in Christ . . . .   1–4.
PART II. Development of unbelief in Israel . . . . . .   5–12.
PART III. Development of faith in the disciples . . . . . 13–21.

I JOHN: JOY IN THE CERTAINTY OF LIFE IN CHRIST, 1–5.

II JOHN: WARNINGS AGAINST ERRORISTS.

III JOHN: EXHORTATION TO STEADFASTNESS.

REVELATION: THE FUTURE OF CHRIST'S KINGDOM.
PART I. Letters to the Seven Churches . . . .   1–3.
PART II. The Seven Seals . . . .   4–7.
PART III. The Seven Trumpets . . . .   8–11.
PART IV. The Seven Mystic Figures . . . .   12–14.
PART V. The Seven Bowls . . . .   15–16.
PART VI. Doom of the Foes of Christ . . . .   17–20.
PART VII. The Blessed Consummation . . . .   21–22.

DIVISION OF THE BIBLE.

Subject: History of Redemption.

I. The Old Testament (Covenant): Redemption prepared.
II. The New Testament (Covenant): Redemption completed.

THE BOOKS OF THE OLD TESTAMENT.

I. Pentateuch, or Law of Moses. 5
1. Genesis.   3. Leviticus.
2. Exodus.   4. Numbers.
5. Deuteronomy.
II. Historical Books. 9.
1. The first three, Joshua, Judges and Ruth.
2. The three double books, Samuel, Kings and Chronicles.
3. The last three, Ezra, Nehemiah and Esther.

III. Poetical Books. 5.
1. Job.   3. Proverbs.
2. Psalms.   4. Ecclesiastes.
   5. Song of Solomon.
IV. Prophetical Books. 12.
   A. Major Prophets.
1. Isaiah.   3. Ezekiel.
2. Jeremiah.   4. Daniel.
   B. Minor Prophets.
1. Hosea.   7. Nahum.
2. Joel.   8. Habakkuk.
3. Amos.   9. Zephaniah.
4. Obadiah.   10. Haggai.
5. Jonah.   11. Zechariah.
6. Micah.   12. Malachi.

Minor Prophets. Ho. Jo. Am.
                Ob. Jo. Mi. Na.
                Ha. Ze. Ha. Ze. Ma.

OUTLINES AND ANALYSES

OF

BIBLE BOOKS AND HISTORY.

FIRST STAGE: The Theocracy, 4004–1095.
Genesis 1 to I Samuel 7.

Genesis.

EPOCH I. PRIMITIVE WORLD, GEN. 1–11.

1. AGE OF ADAM, Gen. 1–5.

Hurlbut, Pa. 17–22.

1. Creation of the world, 1 : 2 : 3.
   a) 1–13. Inorganic history: First three days.
   b) 14–31. Organic history: 4th, 5th and 6th days.
   c) 2 : 1–3. God's day of rest: Seventh day.
2. Creation of man.
   a) 4–18. Eden, man's first home.
   b) 18–25. Woman, man's companion.
3. The fall of man.
   a) 1–6. The disobedience.
   b) 7–21. The curse.
   c) 22–24. The expulsion.
4. Cain and Abel.
   a) 1–15. Cain the fratricide.
   b) 16–24. Cain the fugitive.
   c) 25–26. Birth of Seth in place of Abel.
5. Genealogy of the Sethites or Macrobioi.

2. AGE OF NOAH, Gen. 6-11.

Hurlbut: Pa. 23-27.
6. Preparation for the flood.
   a) 1-8. Universal sinfulness of man.
   b) 9-22. Noah and his commission to build the ark.
7. Coming and prevalence of the flood.
   a) 1-5. Noah's entrance into the ark.
   b) 6-16. Noah's companions.
   c) 17-24. Universal destruction.
8. The end of the flood.
   a) 1-14. The abating of the waters.
   b) 15-22. The saved and thankful race.
9. History of Noah and his family after the flood.
   a) 1-7. The Blessing or original moral law.
   b) 8-17. God's covenant of mercy with him.
   c) 18-29. Conduct of his sons or curse and blessing.
10. Table of nations.
    a) 1-5. Sons of Japheth.
    b) 6-14. Sons of Ham.
    c) 15-20. Sons of Canaan.
    d) 21-32. Sons of Shem.
11. History of mankind from death of Noah to call of Abraham.
    a) 1-9. Dispersion of mankind.
    b) 10-26. Genealogy from Shem to Terah.
    c) 27-32. Terah and his migrations.

EPOCH II. HEBREW PATRIARCHS.

Hurlbut, Pa., 29-36.

3. AGE OF ABRAHAM, Gen. 12-25:18.

12. Abraham's call and migration.
    a) 1-9. His call and journey to Canaan.
    b) 10-20. His sojourn in Egypt.
13. Separation of Abraham and Lot.
14. Meeting of Abraham and Melchizedek.
    a) 1-12. The war in the plain.
    b) 13-24. Rescue of Lot, meeting of Melchizedek.
15. The covenant of faith.
    a) 1-8. God's promise to Abraham.
    b) 9-21. Confirmation of the promise.
16. Ishmael and Hagar.
    a) 1-6. Flight of Hagar.
    b) 7-16. Birth of Ishmael.
17. Covenant of circumcision. Promise of Isaac.
    a) 1-14. Covenant sealed by circumcision.
    b) 15-27. Isaac promised.
18. Abraham visited by the angels.
    a) 1-15. Entertainment of the angels.
    b) 16-33. Abraham's intercession for Sodom.
19. Destruction of Sodom and Gomorrah.
    a) 1-11. Wickedness of the Sodomites.
    b) 12-29. Rescue of Lot and his daughters.
    c) 30-38. Origin of Moab and Ammon.
20. Abraham's deception at Gerar.

21. Isaac, Ishmael and Abimelech.
    a) 1-8. Birth of Isaac.
    b) 9-21. Expulsion of Ishmael.
    c) 22-34. Covenant with Abimelech.
22. Trial of Abraham's faith. Nahor's family.
    a) 1-19. The trial; sacrifice of Isaac.
    b) 20-24. Account of Nahor's family.
23. Death and burial of Sarah.
24. Marriage of Isaac and Rebecca.
    a) 1-29. Abraham sends his servant to Haran.
    b) 30-60. Laban's reception of the servant.
    c) 61-67. Marriage of Isaac and Rebecca.
25 : 1-18. Close of Abraham's life. Ishmael's sons.
    a) 1-11. Abraham's second marriage and death.
    b) 12-18. Ishmael's descendants.

4. AGE OF ISAAC AND JACOB, 25 : 19-36.

25 : 19-34 Boyhood of Esau and Jacob.
    a) 19-26. Circumstances of their birth.
    b) 27-34. Their character.
26. Isaac and Abimelech.
    a) 1-14. Isaac's denial of his wife.
    b) 15-35. Strife over the wells by the servants.
27. Isaac blessing his sons.
    a) 1-29. Jacob stealing Esau's blessing.
    b) 30-46. Esau's blessing and hatred of Jacob.
28. Jacob's flight from home.
    a) 1-9. Isaac sending Jacob to Padan Aram.
    b) 10-22. Jacob at Bethel.
29. Leah and Rachel. Leah's first four sons.
    a) 1-14. Jacob's meeting with Rachel.
    b) 15-30. Jacob's marriages with Leah and Rachel.
    c) 31-35. Jacob and Leah's first four sons.
30. Jacob's concubines and wealth.
    a) 1-24. The concubines Bilhah and Silpah.
    b) 25-43. Jacob's bargain with Laban and his wealth.
31. Jacob's departure for Canaan.
    a) 1-21. Consultation with his wives and departure.
    b) 22-43. Contention between Jacob and Laban.
    c) 44-55. Their treaty of peace.
32. Jacob's fear of Esau and wrestling with God.
    a) 1-21. Jacob's reconciling presents for Esau.
    b) 22-32. Jacob's wrestling with God at Jabbok.
33. Reconciliation of Jacob and Esau. Jacob at Shechem.
    a) 1-17. The meeting and reconciliation.
    b) 18-20. Jacob's settlement at Shechem.
34. Defilement of Dinah by Shechem.
    a) 1-12. Hamor's proposal to intermarry.
    b) 13-24. The terms of agreement.
    c) 25-31. The treachery of Simeon and Levi.
35. Jacob's journeys from Shechem to Hebron.
    a) 1-8. Journeys from Shechem to Luz.
    b) 9-22. Rachel's death from travail with Benjamin.
    c) 23-29. Jacob's return to Hebron. Burial of Isaac.
36. Appendix: Esau's descendants.
    a) 1-19. Sons of Esau and their dukes.
    b) 20-30. Sons of Seir, the Horite.
    c) 31-43. The kings of Edom.

5. AGE OF JOSEPH, or ISRAEL IN BONDAGE, 37–50.

  a) History of Joseph, 37–45.
37. Joseph sold into Egypt.
    a) 1–12. Joseph envied by his brothers.
    b) 13–36. Joseph plotted against and sold.
38. Judah and Tamar.
    a) 1–11. Judah's injustice towards Tamar.
    b) 12–30. Tamar's revenge on Judah.
39. Joseph's stewardship and imprisonment
    a) 1–6. His stewardship in the house of Potiphar.
    b) 7–12. His temptation by Potiphar's wife.
    c) 13–23. His false accusation and imprisonment.
40. Joseph interpreting the dreams of the butler and baker.
    a) 1–15. The butler's dream interpreted.
    b) 16–23. The baker's dream; fulfilment of the dreams.
41. Pharaoh's dream and Joseph's exaltation.
    a) 1–37. The dream and its meaning.
    b) 38–57. Joseph vice-regent of Egypt.
42. The first journey of Jacob's sons to Egypt.
    a) 1–17. Their imprisonment as spies.
    b) 18–38. Their release and return home.
43. Second journey of Jacob's sons to Egypt.
    a) 1–14. Their long-delayed journey.
    b) 15–34. Their reception by Joseph.
44. The pretended charge of theft against Benjamin.
    a) 1–17. Departure and arrest of Benjamin.
    b) 18–34. Judah's intercession for Benjamin.
45. Joseph's revelation of himself.
    a) 1–15. The revelation.
    b) 16–28. The return of Jacob's sons with the news.
46. Descent of Jacob and his family to Egypt.
    a) 1–7. The descent to Egypt.
    b) 8–27. The family register.
    c) 28–34. Meeting of Jacob and Joseph.
47. Settlement in Goshen. Joseph's political wisdom. Jacob's sickness.
    a) 1–12. Settlement in Goshen.
    b) 13–27. Joseph's political economy.
    c) 28–31. Jacob's sickness.
48. Jacob blessing Ephraim and Manasseh.
    a) 1–11. Jacob's review of God's dealings.
    b) 12–22. The blessing on Joseph's sons.
49. Jacob's parting blessings and death.
    a) 1–27. His blessings on his sons.
    b) 28–33. His death.
50. Jacob's burial and Joseph's death.
    a) 1–13. Jacob's honorable burial.
    b) 14–21. Joseph feared by his brethren.
    c) 22–26. Joseph's death.

THE BOOK OF JOB.

Part I. THE PROLOGUE, 1–2.

1. The man Job and his first trial.
    a) 1–5. Home and character of Job.
    b) 6–12. Job's religious sincerity questioned by Satan.
    c) 13–22. Job's first trial and its issue.

2. Job's second trial and the visit of his friends.
    a) 1–10. Job's second trial and its issue.
    b) 11–13. The visit and condolence of his friends.

Part II. THE DISCUSSION, 3–31.

3. The occasion: Job's complaining of his life.
    a) 1–10. His wish never to have been conceived or born.
    b) 11–19. His wish to have died at his birth.
    c) 20–26. Complaint that the wretched should live.
    §1. The first circle of speeches, 4–14.
    Argument: General idea of God proves Job punished for sin.

Speech of Eliphaz, Job reproved for murmuring.

4. Relation between God and the righteous man.
    a) 1–11. He never perishes under affliction.
    b) 12–21. He does not oppose God's holy ways.
5. Warning and admonition to Job.
    a) 1–7. A warning against Job's murmuring.
    b) 8–16. God's purpose of goodness in all his ways.
    c) 17–26. Application: Appeal to Job to turn to God.

Job's reply to Eliphaz, 6–7.

6. Self-defense and complaint against his friends.
    a) 1–13. Defense of the violence of his complaint.
    b) 14–30. Disappointed at the position of his friends.
7. Renewed outburst at the thought of his destiny, 1–21.

Speech of Bildad.

8. Defense of God against Job's attack.
    a) 1–7. God's justice.
    b) 8–19. The moral wisdom of the ancients.
    c) 20–22. The principle of divine justice applied to Job's case.

Job's reply to Bildad, 9–10.

9. Man's helplessness in a plea with a mighty and a terrible God.
    a) 1–10. God's omnipotence as seen in nature.
    b) 11–24. Man's helplessness in God's presence.
    c) 25–35. Job's view of his own condition.
10. Job's appeal to God for the reason of his suffering.
    a) 1–12. Can it be that God despises the work of his own hands.
    b) 13–19. If Job is so wicked, why does God let him live?
    c) 20–22. His desire that God give him rest for his short term of life.

Speech of Zophar.

11. Appeal to divine wisdom and power to show Job his hidden sin.
    a) 1–6. Desire that God would show Job his wisdom.
    b) 7–12. Praise of the divine wisdom.
    c) 13–20. Exhortation to Job to put away his evil.

Job's reply to Zophar, 12–14.

12. Job's knowledge of God's wisdom and power.
    a) 1–6. His own case a contradiction to the principle of retribution.
    b) 7–25. His own knowledge of God's wisdom and power.
13. Job's rebuke of his friends and plea with God.
    a) 1–12. The rebuke to his friends.
    b) 13–22. His desire to plead his case with God.
    c) 23–28. Job pleading his case with God.

14. Job's plea for mankind.
    a) 1–6. Shortness of life a plea for freedom from trouble.
    b) 7–12. Man's irretrievable death a plea for rest.
    c) 13–22. Job's longing for another life.
    §2. Second circle of speeches, 15–21.
    Argument against Job from God's providence.

    SECOND SPEECH OF ELIPHAZ.
15. Rebuke of and instruction for Job.
    a) 2–16. Rebuke of Job's self-exaltation and irreverence.
    b) 17–35. Eliphaz's doctrine of the wicked's feelings and fate.

    JOB'S REPLY TO ELIPHAZ, 16–17.
16. Job's complaint and appeal to earth.
    a) 2–5. Complaint of the weariness of his friends' speeches.
    b) 6–17. A picture of his desolate condition.
    c) 18–17:2. An appeal to earth not to cover his blood.
17. Appeal to God and rejection of the proffered hope.
    a) 3–9. Appeal to God to be Job's surety with himself.
    b) 10–16. Job's hopeless outlook.

    SECOND SPEECH OF BILDAD.
18. Bildad's view of the wicked man's fate.
    a) 2–4. His astonishment at Job's talk.
    b) 5–21. History of the wicked man's downfall.

    JOB'S REPLY TO BILDAD.
19. The conflict of Job's thoughts on God.
    a) 2–6. Complaint against the heartlessness of his friends.
    b) 7–12. God's desertion of and hostility to him.
    c) 13–22. God has turned all men against him.
    d) 23–27. Job's dim hope from God for the future.
    e) 28–29. Threat against his friends.

    ZOPHAR'S SECOND SPEECH.
20. The brevity of the wicked man's prosperity.
    a) 1–3. Zophar's indignation at Job.
    b) 4–12. Brevity of the wicked man's prosperity.
    c) 13–22. His sin brings its own retribution.
    d) 23–29. Sinner's greed sated with God's judgment.

    JOB'S REPLY TO ZOPHAR.
21. The wicked's prosperity is the great mystery of providence.
    a) 2–6. Job's request to be heard.
    b) 7–16. The fact that the wicked are prosperous.
    c) 17–21. The fact that the wicked are seldom struck by calamity.
    d) 22–26. It is a mystery of God.
    e) 27–34. Rebuke to his friend's ignorant insinuations.
    §3. Third circle of speeches, 22–31.
    Direct assertions of Job's deserving guilt.

    THIRD SPEECH OF ELIPHAZ.
22. Job directly charged with great sinfulness.
    a) 1–5. Charge of great iniquity.
    b) 6–11. Supposed sins of Job.
    c) 12–20. Supposed motive of Job's sinning.
    d) 21–30. Job exhorted to be reconciled with God.

Job's Reply to Eliphaz, 23–24.

23. His mysterious injustice at the hand of God.
    a) 2–7. His desire to find God and plead with him.
    b) 8–12. God's evasions of the innocent plaintiff.
    c) 13–17. God's arbitrary, mysterious dealings with Job.
24. God's failures in the righteous government of the world.
    a) 2–12. His failure to punish high-handed iniquity.
    b) 13–25. His maintaining secret sinners.

Third Speech of Bildad.

25. 1–26. God's exaltation over impure man.

Job's Reply to Bildad, 26–30.

26. God's exaltation no answer to the enigma of Job's suffering.
    a) 2–4. Sarcastic admiration of Bildad's speech.
    b) 5–14. Job's greater appreciation of God's exaltation.
27. Job's affirmation of his own innocence.
    a) 1–6. His solemn assertion of his innocence.
    b) 7–10. The wicked man's troubled state of mind.
    c) 11–23. The wicked man's external destruction.
28. Wisdom [of God's providence (?)] unattainable by man.
    a) 1–12. It is not among the many treasures of earth.
    b) 13–19. Can not be bought at any price.
    c) 20–28. God only knows its place. Man's wisdom is: Fear God.
29. Job's sad review of his former happiness.
    a) 1–10. Survey of his former happy days.
    b) 11–17. His benevolence and impartial justice.
    c) 18–25. His then happy outlook and honor.
30. Contrast between his present pitiable condition with the past.
    a) 1–8. A picture of the base fellows who now despise him.
    b) 9–15. The indignities he suffers from them.
    c) 16–23. His present miserable condition.
    d) 24–31. The heart-rending contrast between then and now.
31. Job's solemn assurance of his innocence.
    a) 1–12. Innocence of sensual desire.
    b) 13–23. Innocence of sin of oppression.
    c) 24–31. Innocence of secret sinful emotions.
    d) 32–41. Assertion of his innocence.

Part III. THE SPEECHES OF ELIHU, 32–37.

32. Elihu's reasons for taking part in the discussion.
    a) 1–5. Elihu introduced.
    b) 6–22. His reason for taking part, to justify God.
33. Denial of Job's assertion that God is arbitrarily hostile to him.
    a) 1–7. Reason why Job should listen to him, a youth.
    b) 8–13. Nature of God forbids the idea of divine injustice.
    c) 14–28. God's ways of speaking to man. cf. Heb. 12: 5, 7, 11.
    d) 29–33. Job invited to reply.
34. Denial of Job's assertion that God is unjust to him.
    a) 1–9. Address to the friends and statement of the question.
    b) 10–30. Examination and refutation of Job's opinion.
    c) 31–37. Appeal to Job to confess his sins.
35. Refutation of Job's assertion that piety is useless.
    a) 1–8. A supreme God is untouched by man's sins or piety.
    b) 9–16. Reasons for the unanswered prayers of the righteous.

36. God's gracious designs in afflicting man.
    a) 1-15. God's gracious wisdom even in affliction.
    b) 16-25. Application of the principle to Job's case.
37. Lessons for Job from the greatness of God in nature.
    a) 36 : 26–37 : 13. Marvelous greatness of God in the work of nature.
    b) 14-24. God's superiority over us should engender confidence.

PART IV. JEHOVAH'S ANSWER TO JOB, 38–42 : 6.

38. Survey of inanimate nature.
    a) 1-11. Earth and sea.
    b) 12-18. The dawn and the ocean depth.
    c) 19-38. The wonders of the heavens.
39. Survey of the animal world.
    a) 38 : 39–39 : 4. Lion, raven, wild goats and hinds.
    b) 5-18. Wild ass, wild ox and ostrich.
    c) 19-30. The war horse, the hawk and the eagle.
40. Effect of God's first speech. Opening of the second.
    a) 1-5. Effect of God's speech on Job.
    b) 6-14. Job ironically requested to rule the world.
    c) 15-24. The Behemoth, can he rule so much as him?
41. The Leviathan : i. e., Crocodile, can he rule it?
    a) 1-11. Impossibility of capturing it.
    b) 12-34. Description of its parts.
42. Job's answer. Epilogue : Job's prosperity.
    a) 1-6. Job's answer to God.
        Epilogue.
    b) 7-17. Job's twofold prosperity.
    6. THE AGE OF MOSES. Ex., Lev., Num., Deut.
        Hurlbut, Pa. 41-50.

EXODUS: DELIVERANCE AND ESTABLISHMENT OF ISRAEL.

PART I. DELIVERANCE OF ISRAEL FROM EGYPT, 1-18.

§1. Preparation for deliverance, 1-6.
1. Oppression of Israel in Egypt.
    a) 1-7. Increase of Jacob's posterity.
    b) 8-14. Attempt to check the increase by hard labor.
    c) 15-22. Reproof of much wives and attempt by killing the sons.
2. The early life of Moses.
    a) 1-10. Birth and preservation.
    b) 11-12. Flight into Midian.
    c) 23-25. God's recognition of Israel's suffering.
3. Call of Moses at the burning bush.
    a) 1-10. Moses' call and commission to go to Pharaoh.
    b) 11-22. God urges him to go in spite of his objections.
4. Moses' final acceptance of the call.
    a) 1-17. Moses' reluctant acceptance of the work.
    b) 18-26. Moses' return to Egypt.
    c) 27-31. Aaron sent to meet Moses.
5. The opening of the conflict for deliverance.
    a) 1-5. Moses and Aaron demand the freedom of Israel.
    b) 6-18. Pharaoh increases the people's burdens.
    c) 19-23. The people's complaint against Moses.

6. Moses reassured by God. His charge and ancestry.
    a) 1–9. Moses reassured of God's help.
    b) 10–13. God's charge to Moses to go to Pharaoh and the people.
    c) 14–30. Moses' ancestry.
    §2. Miraculous deliverance from Egypt, 7–14.
7. Moses' wonders before Pharaoh and the first plague.
    a) 1–7. Moses told to go before the king.
    b) 8–13. The miracle of the rod.
    c) 14–25. The first plague, bloody waters.
8. The second, third and fourth plagues.
    a) 1–15. The second plague, frogs.
    b) 16 19. The third plague, fleas or lice.
    c) 20–32. The fourth plague, flies.
9. The fifth, sixth and seventh plagues.
    a) 1–7. The fifth plague, murrain.
    b) 8–12. The sixth plague, blains or boils.
    c) 13–35. The seventh plague, hail.
10. The eighth and ninth plagues.
    a) 1–11. Description of the plague of locusts.
    b) 12–20. The eighth plague, locusts.
    c) 21–29. The ninth plague, darkness.
11. 1–10. The forewarning of the tenth plague.
12. The tenth or last plague and final deliverance.
    a) 1–20. The institution of the Passover.
    b) 21–28. Moses commands Elders to kill the Passover.
    c) 29–36. Tenth plague, death of the first born.
    d) 37–51. Israel's departure from Rameses to Succoth.
13. Memorial institutions. Journey from Succoth to Etham.
    a) 1–10. Institution of the days of unleavened bread.
    b) 11–16. Setting apart of the first born.
    c) 17–22. Journey from Succoth to Etham.
14. Victorious passage through the Red Sea.
    a) 1–14. Israel's distress at the Red Sea.
    b) 15–25. Israel's passage through the sea followed by Egypt.
    c) 26–31. Destruction of Egyptians in the sea.
    §3. March of Israel from the Red Sea to Sinai, 15–18.
15. Song of Moses and the march to Elim.
    a) 1–21. Song of Moses.
    b) 22–27. March from Red Sea to Elim.
16. The quails and the manna.
    a) 1–20. The feeding of the hungering people.
    b) 21–36. The manna and the Sabbath.
17. Smiting of the rock. Battle with Ameleck.
    a) 1–7. Smiting the rock for water.
    b) 8–16. Smiting of Amelek at Rephidim.
18. Moses visited by Jethro, his father-in-law.
    a) 1–12. Meeting of Jethro and Moses.
    b) 13–27. Appointment of assistants for Moses.

PART II. GOD'S COVENANT WITH THE NEW NATION, ISRAEL, 19–40.

    §1. The laws of the covenant, 19–24.
19. Preparation of the people for accepting the law.
    a) 1–18. People's agreement with God.
    b) 9–15. Preparations for meeting God.
    c) 16–25. God's meeting the people.

20. Constitutional principles of the covenant.
    a) 1–17. The Decalogue.
    b) 18–26. General principle of divine worship.
21. Laws against personal injuries.
    a) 1–11. Laws of personal liberty.
    b) 12–27. Laws against (personal) harms done.
    c) 28–32. Laws against a goring ox.
22. Laws concerning possessions.
    a) 21 : 33–22 : 6. Laws for the security of property.
    b) 7–15. Laws concerning trusts.
    c) 16–19. Laws against witchcraft and immorality.
    d) 20–31. Sacrifices, usury, first fruits.
23. Laws concerning personal rights.
    a) 1–13. Laws concerning another's rights.
    b) 14–19. Religious rights.
    c) 20–33. Blessings for serving Jehovah.
24. The sealing of the covenant.
    a) 1–11. Sprinkling of the "blood of the covenant."
    b) 12–18. Deliverance of the tables to Moses.
        §2. Divine directions for making the Tabernacle, 25–31.
25. Directions for making the furniture of it.
    a) 1–9. Directions for the material in general.
    b) 10–22. The pattern of the ark of the covenant.
    c) 23–30. The pattern of the table of show bread, 23–30.
    d) 31–40. The pattern of the candlestick.
26. Directions for the Tabernacle itself.
    a) 1–14. The curtains.
    b) 15–30. The boards.
    c) 31–37. The veil.
27. Directions for the great altar, outer court, oil for burning.
    a) 1–8. The altar of burnt offering.
    b) 9–19. The outer court.
    c) 20–21. The oil for the lamp.
28. Directions for the garments of the priests.
    a) 1–5. General directions.
    b) 6–12. The ephod.
    c) 13–30. The breast plate of judgment.
    d) 31–35. The robe of the ephod.
    e) 36–43. Frontlets, coats, girdles, breeches.
29. Directions for dedicating the priests and altar. Daily sacrifices.
    a) 1–37. Dedication of the priests and altar.
    b) 38–46. Daily burnt offerings of the priests.
30. Directions for other belongings of the Tabernacle.
    a) 1–10. The altar of incense.
    b) 11–16. Half-shekel tribute for Jehovah.
    c) 17–21. The laver.
    d) 22–33. The holy anointing oil.
    e) 34–38. Incense.
31. Directions concerning the workmen. Sabbath law.
    a) 1–11. The workmen for the Tabernacle.
    b) 12–17. Inculcation of the Sabbath law.
    c) 18. The tables of the law given to Moses.
        §3. The breaking and restoration of the covenant, 32–34.
32. The idolatry of the golden calf.
    a) 1–6. The making of the image.
    b) 7–14. God's wrath and Moses' intercession.
    c) 15–29. Moses' anger against and punishment of the sin.
    d) 30–35. Moses' atonement for the sin of the people.

33. Consequences of the sin.
    a) 1–6. God's refusal to lead the people.
    b) 7–11. The "tent of meeting" put outside the camp.
    c) 12–23. Moses' desire to see God.
34. Restoration of the covenant.
    a) 1–9. Revelation of God's character to Moses.
    b) 10–28. Renewal of the covenant. Restatement of its laws.
    c) 29–35. Moses' descent from the mount with shining face.
      §4. Construction of the Tabernacle and belongings, 35–40.
      Hurlbut. Pages 135–139.
35. Preparation for the work of building.
    a) 1–3. Six days the time for work.
    b) 4–19. The people commanded to bring material.
    c) 20–29. The people's free will offerings.
    d) 30–36:1. The calling of the workmen.
36. Construction of the Tabernacle proper.
    a) 2–7. The surplus material.
    b) 8–19. The making of the covering.
    c) 20–34. The making of the boards.
    d) 35–38. The making of the veils or curtains.
37. Construction of the furniture in the Tabernacle, viz.:
    a) 1–9. The ark of the covenant.
    b) 10–16. The table of show bread.
    c) 17–24. The candlestick.
    d) 25–29. The altar of incense.
38. The altar and laver with outer court. Accounts.
    a) 1–8. Construction of the great altar.
    b) 9–20. Construction of the outer court.
    c) 21–31. Summary account of metals used.
39. The making of the priestly garments.
    a) 1–7. The ephod.
    b) 8–21. The breast plate.
    c) 22–32. The minor articles of dress.
    d) 33–43. Moses' approval of the work.
40. Erection and dedication of the Tabernacle.
    a) 1–16. Erection at God's command.
    b) 17–33. Arrangement of the furniture.
    c) 34–38. Dedication by God's presence.

LEVITICUS. CEREMONIAL LAWS.

PART I. LAWS CONCERNING SACRIFICES, 1–7.

1. The burnt offering, consisting of:
    a) 1–9. A male of the herd.
    b) 10–13. A male of the flock.
    c) 14–17. A fowl.
2. The meal offering in form.
    a) 1–3. Uncooked.
    b) 4–10. Cooked.
    c) 11–13. First fruits.
3. Peace (thank) offering, consisting of:
    a) 1–5. One of the herd.
    b) 6–11. One of the flock, a sheep.
    c) 12–17. Of a goat of the flock.

4. The law of sin offering.
    a) 1–12. For the priest.
    b) 13–21. For the whole congregation.
    c) 22–26. For a ruler.
    d) 27–35. One of the commoners.
5. 6: 7 Heb. 5. Sins demanding sin offering.
    a) 1–6. Connivance at swearing, uncleanness, swearing.
    b) 7–13. Modification of offer in favor of the poor.
    c) 14–16. Unfaithfulness in the sacred tribute.
    d) 17–22. Sins of ignorance.
    e) 6: 1–7. Sins of dishonesty.
6. Laws of the burnt offering, meal offering, oblation and sin offering.
    a) 8–13 [6: 1-6]. The laws of the burnt offering.
    b) 14–18 [6: 7–11]. The laws of the meal offering.
    c) 19 23 [6: 12–16]. Aaron's oblation.
    d) 24–30 [6: 17-23]. The laws of the sin offering.
7. Laws of the guilt and peace offering. Use of fats.
    a) 1–10. Of the guilt offering.
    b) 11–21. Of the peace offering.
    c) 22–38. General directions for the use of fats.

PART II. HISTORICAL. INAUGURATION OF THE PRIESTHOOD, 8–10.

8. Consecration of Aaron and his sons.
    a) 1–13. Their clothing and anointing.
    b) 14–30. Their sacrifices.
    c) 31–36. Instruction for the priests.
9. The entrance of the priests on their office.
    a) 1–7. Aaron's instructions and sin offering.
    b) 8–15. Aaron's offering the burnt offering.
10. Death of Nadab and Abihu. Priestly precepts.
    a) 1–7. Death of Nadab and Abihu.
    b) 8–15. Precepts concerning wine and eating.
    c) 16–20. Exceptions to eating the meat of the sin offering.

PART III. LAWS OF PURIFICATION. DAY OF ATONEMENT, 11–16.

11. Things that make unclean by eating or touching.
    a) 1–23. By eating specified beasts of the earth, fishes, fowls, creepers.
    b) 24–47. By touching any carcase or specified living thing.
12. Purification in cases of confinement, 1–8.
13. Laws concerning leprosy.
    a) 1–46. Six cases of leprosy in human beings.
    b) 47–59. Leprosy in clothing.
14. Purification of lepers. Leprous houses.
    a) 1–20. Purification of the leper.
    b) 21–32. Provision for the poor leper.
    c) 33–57. Leprous houses.
15. Uncleanness by issues.
    a) 1–18. Issue of semen virile.
    b) 19–33. Woman's blood issue.
16. Day of atonement.
    a) 1–19. The victims and atonement for the holy place.
    b) 20–28. The disposing of the two goats.
    c) 29–34. Inculcation of this observance.

PART IV. LAWS FOR ISRAEL AS GOD'S HOLY PEOPLE, 17-27.

17. The law of offering sacrifices.
    a) 1-9. The place for killing the sacrifice.
    b) 10-16. The use of the blood.
18. Marriage and chastity laws.
    a) 1-5. God's claim to obedience of his laws.
    b) 6-23. Precepts against lust and unlawful marriage.
    c) 24-30. Exhortation to keep these precepts.
19. Laws for religious, civil and moral life.
    a) 1-13. Duties to superiors: fifth commandment.
    b) 14-25. Civil laws.
    c) 26-37. Sunday prohibitions.
20. Punishments for sins of uncleanness.
    a) 1-21. The sins and their punishment.
    b) 22-27. The necessity of keeping these laws.
21. Precepts concerning the purity of the priests.
    a) 1-15. The command to be pure.
    b) 16-24. Bodily formation of the priests.
22. Concerning holy things and sacrifices.
    a) 1-16. The partakers of holy things.
    b) 17-25. The character of sacrifices.
    c) 26-33. Three further precepts for sacrifices.
23. Laws for celebrating feasts.
    a) 1-8. The Sabbath and the passover.
    b) 9-22. Feast of first fruits and pentecost.
    c) 23-32. Feast of trumpets and day of atonement.
    d) 33-44. Feast of Tabernacles.
24. Miscellaneous precepts.
    a) 1-9. Precepts for care of Tabernacle furniture.
    b) 10-23. Against blaspheming and so forth.
25. Holy years.
    a) 1-24. Sabbatical year and year of jubilee.
    b) 25-55. Land tenure in view of jubilee.
26. Promises and threats.
    a) 1-13. Promised blessings on obedience.
    b) 14-26. Humiliation threatened on disobedience.
    c) 27-46. Total destruction impending disobedience.
27. Vows, devoted things and tithes.
    a) 1-25. Vows.
    b) 26-29. Devoted things.
    c) 30-34. Tithes.

NUMBERS. ISRAEL'S LIFE IN THE WILDERNESS.

PART I. PREPARATION FOR DEPARTURE FROM SINAI, 1-9.

1. Numbers of the men fit for war.
    a) 1-19. Appointment of enumerators.
    b) 20-31. Census of Reuben, Simeon, Gad, Judah, Issa., Zeb.
    c) 32-43. Census of Ephra., Manas., Benj., Dan, Assher, Napht.
    d) 45-54. Remarks on the census. The Levites.
2. Order and arrangement of the camp.
    a) 1-9. The east or van, Judah, Issachar and Zebulon.
    b) 10-16. The south or right wing, Reuben, Simeon, Gad.
    c) 17-24. The rear or west, Ephraim, Manasseh and Benjamin.
    d) 25-34. The north or left wing, Dan, Assher, Naphtali.

3. General assignment of the work of Levites.
    a) 1–20. Choice and charge of the tribe of Levi.
    b) 21–39. Number and charge of the families Gershom, Kohath, Merari.
    c) 40–51. Redemption of the overplus first-born Israelites.
4. Special assignment of work to families, viz.:
    a) 1–20. To the family of Kohath.
    b) 21–28. To the family of Gershom.
    c) 29–33. To the family of Merari.
    d) 35–49. Census of these families.
5. Laws of cleanliness, atonement and jealousy.
    a) 1–4. Laws of camp cleanliness.
    b) 5–10. Restitution for atonement of.
    c) 11–31. Laws for trial of suspected wife.
6. Law of the Nazarite and form of blessing.
    a) 1–12. Requirements of the Nazarite.
    b) 13–21. Laws for fulfillment of a vow.
    c) 22–27. Aaronite benediction.
7. Dedication gifts of the tribal princes.
    a) 1–11. The gift of six ox teams.
    b) 12–29. The gifts of the princes Judah, Issachar, Zebulon.
    c) 30–47. The gifts of the princes Reuben, Simeon, Gad.
    d) 48–56. The gifts of the princes Dan, Assher, Naphtali.
    e) 66–83. The gifts of the princes Ephraim, Manasseh, Benjamin.
    f) 84–89. Summary of all the gifts.
8. Consecration of all the Levites.
    a) 1–4. Directions for lighting the lamp.
    b) 5–22. Consecration of the Levites.
    c) 23–26. Age and time of service of the Levites.
9. Second passovers, guiding pillar of cloud and fire.
    a) 1–14. Observance of second passovers.
    b) 15–23. The guidance of the pillar.

PART II. JOURNEY OF ISRAEL FROM SINAI TO MOAB, 10–21.

    §1. Journey from Sinai to Kadesh Barnea, 10–14.
    Hurlbut: Pa., 37–40.
10. Israel's departure from Sinai.
    a) 1–10. Silver signal trumpets.
    b) 11–28. The order of the march.
    c) 29–32. Hobab's alliance with Israel.
    d) 33–36. Signal words for the march.
11. Moses' troubles at Taberah.
    a) 1–4. Murmurings punished by fire.
    b) 5–15. Lusting after the flesh-pots of Egypt.
    c) 16–29. The assistant elders.
    d) 30–35. The quails and the graves of lust.
12. 1–16. Miriam's rebellion and leprosy.
13. The spying out of the land of Canaan.
    a) 1–16. The names of the spies.
    b) 17–24. The work of the spies.
    c) 25–33. The unfavorable report of the spies.
14. Rebellion and punishment of the people.
    a) 1–10. The discontent of the people.
    b) 11–25. The softening of the threatened punishment.
    c) 26–45. Exclusion of adults from Canaan.
    §2. The wanderings in the wilderness, 15–19.

15. Laws for sacrifices, Sabbaths and tassels.
    a) 1-21. Laws for sacrifices and offering for all.
    b) 22-31. Atonements for sins of ignorance.
    c) 32-41. Sabbath breaker [32-36] tassels.
16. Rebellion of Korah, Dathan, Abiram.
    a) 1-19. Their rebellion.
    b) 20-35. Death of the rebels.
    c) 36-40. Censers of the rebels as memorials, Heb. 17 : 5.
    d) 41-50. The murmurings and punishment of Israel.
17. 1-13. The budding of Aaron's rod.
18. Service and perquisites of the priest and Levites.
    a) 1-7. Services of the priests and Levites.
    b) 8-20. Perquisites of the priests.
    c) 21-24. Perquisites of the Levites.
    d) 25-32. Contributions of Levites to the priests.
19. The red heifer
    a) 1-9. Preparation of the purifying water.
    b) 10-22. Direction for its use.
    §3 Journey of Israel from Kadesh to Moab, 20-21.
20. Journey from Kadesh to Mt. Hor.
    a) 1-13. Murmurings for water at Meribah.
    b) 14-21. Edom refuses passage to Israel.
    c) 22-29. Journey to Hor and death of Aaron.
21. Journey from Hor to the plains of Moab.
    a) 1-3. Arad's attack on Israel.
    b) 4-15. Fiery serpents on journey to Arnor.
    c) 16-20. Song of the wells.
    d) 21-35. Sihon and Og.

PART III. EVENTS AND LAWS IN MOAB, 22-36.

22. Balaak's hiring Balaam.
    a) 1-14. Balaak's first attempt to get Balaam.
    b) 15-21. Balaak's second attempt to get Balaam.
    c) 22-35. Balaam rebuked by an angel.
    d) 36-41. Balaam entertained by Balaak.
23. Balaam's vain attempts to curse Israel.
    a) 1-10. His first " Parable."
    b) 11-24. His second " Parable."
    c) 25-30. Balaak's seven altars on Peor.
24. Prediction of the Star out of Jacob.
    a) 1-9. Balaam's third " Parable."
    b) 10-25. Balaam's fourth " Parable ": the coming Star.
25. Baal Peor and the zeal of Phinehas.
    a) 1-9. Israel's participation in idolatry.
    b) 10-15. Zeal of Phinehas for Jehovah rewarded.
    c) 16-18. Divine command to smite Midian.
26. The second census of the men of war.
    a) 1-27. Reuben, Simeon, Gad, Judah, Issachar and Zebulon.
    b) 28-51. Manasseh, Ephraim, Benj., Dan, Assher and Naphtali.
    c) 52-56. Laws for dividing the land.
    d) 57-65. Families of the Levites.
27. Female heirs and the successor of Moses.
    a) 1-11. The laws of female heirs.
    b) 12-23. Joshua as successor of Moses.

28. Various offerings to be observed.
   a) 1–8. The continual burnt offering.
   b) 9–10. Sabbath day offering.
   c) 11–15. New moon offering.
   d) 16–25. Passover offerings.
   e) 26–31. First fruit offerings.
29. Various offerings to be observed continued.
   a) 1–6. At the feast of trumpets.
   b) 7–11. On the day of atonement.
   c) 12–39. The feast of Tabernacles.
30. 1–16. Validity and obligation of vows.
31. Victory over Midian.
   a) 1–12. The slaying of the Midianites.
   b) 13–24. The law concerning plunder.
   c) 25–54. Counting and dividing the spoil.
32. Settlement of Reuben, Gad and half Manasseh.
   a) 1–6. Their request to stay east of Jordan.
   b) 7–15. Moses' disapproval.
   c) 16–27. The conditions of their staying east.
   d) 28–42. Allotment of their land.
33. List of forty journeys. Expulsion of Canaanites.
   a) 1–15. Journeys from Egypt to Sinai.
   b) 16–36. Journeys from Sinai to Kadesh Barnea.
   c) 37–49. Journeys from Kadesh to Moab.
   d) 50–56. Command to expel the Canaanites.
34. Directions for dividing the promised land.
   a) 1–15. The borders of the land.
   b) 16–29. The men who shall divide it.
35. Levitical cities and cities of refuge.
   a) 1–9. Levitical cities.
   b) 10–34. Cities of refuge.
36. 1–13. Law for the marriage of heiresses.

DEUTERONOMY. FAREWELL ADDRESS OF MOSES.

PART I. THE FIRST ADDRESS OF MOSES, 1–4.

§1. Historical review, 1–3.

1. Review of the experience from Horeb to Kadesh.
   a) 1–5. Introduction.
   b) 6–18. God's dealings at Horeb.
   c) 19–46. History of Israel at Kadesh.
2. Review of the history from Kadesh to Jordan and defeat of Sihon.
   a) 1–23. The nations spared by Israel.
   b) 24–37. Israel's victory over Sihon.
3. Conquests made and to be made.
   a) 1–11. Recital of victory over Og, king of Bashan.
   b) 12–17. The first acquisition of land.
   c) 18–22. Possessions on the west of Jordan to be taken.
   d) 23–29. Moses debarred from entering Canaan.

§2. Exhortation, 4.

4. Exhortation to keep the divine laws, and appendix.
   a) 1–8. Exhortation to keep the divine laws generally.
   b) 9–14. Exhortation to keep the ten commandments.
   c) 15–31. Exhortation to realize who God, the lawgiver, is.
   d) 32–40. Exhortation to consider the advantages of these laws.
   e) 41–43. Appendix: East Jordanic cities of refuge.
   f) 44–49. Historical introduction to the second address.

PART II. SECOND ADDRESS, 5-26.

§1. Concerning the first and second commandments, 5-11.
5. The decalogue as text of the address.
    a) 1-5. How it had been given.
    b) 6-21 : 18. The decalogue.
    c) 22 : 18-33 : 30. How Moses had received the laws.
6. Exhortation to love and obey Jehovah.
    a) 1-3. General exhortation.
    b) 4-15. The exhortation to love Jehovah.
    c) 16-25. The command to obey Jehovah.
7. Warnings not to have fellowship with outside nations.
    a) 1-11. Their conduct toward the nations.
    b) 12-16. The reward for obedience.
    c) 17-26. The snares to fellowship.
8. God's dealings towards them in the past is a motive to obey.
    a) 1-10. Reasons for keeping his laws.
    b) 11-20. They shall beware of forgetfulness of the laws.
9. Warnings against self-righteousness.
    a) 1-6. Because there is nothing to boast of.
    b) 7-29. Because there is much to be humble for.
10. An exhortation to be loyal to God.
    a) 1-11. Because he restored the broken covenant.
    b) 12-22. Because he seeks only their own good.
11. Incentives to love and obey God.
    a) 1-7. What he did for them in Egypt and the wilderness.
    b) 8-12. That they may be able to hold the promised land.
    c) 13-25. That they may be able to reap the blessings of the law.
    d) 26-32. The alternative is the curse.

§2. Particular laws, 12-26.
12. The central sanctuary.
    a) 1-7. Command to destroy heathen shrines.
    b) 8-14. Precepts concerning the place and manner of sacrifice.
    c) 15-28. Non sacrificial or ordinary feasts.
    d) 29-32. Warnings against imitating idolators.
13. Command to punish idolatry.
    a) 1-5. In general cases.
    b) 6-11. Even in case of a near relative.
    c) 12-18. In case of a city.
14. Heathen funeral customs. Clean and unclean. Tithes.
    a) 1-2. Heathen funeral customs prohibited.
    b) 3-21. Clean and unclean food.
    c) 22-29. Tithes.
15. Year of jubilee and firstlings of cattle.
    a) 1-11. The year of release of debt.
    b) 12-18. Release of the Hebrew bondman.
    c) 19-23. Firstlings of the cattle.
16. Annual feasts. Principles of justice. Sacrifice.
    a) 1-17. The passover, feast of weeks and of tabernacles.
    b) 18-20. General principles of justice.
    c) 21-17 : 1. Laws of sacrifice.
17. Judicial and executive officers.
    a) 2-7. Command to punish idolatrous persons.
    b) 8-13. Priests and Levites are to form supreme court.
    c) 14-20. The future king.

18. Concerning priests, Levites and prophets.
    a) 1–5. Concerning priests' portions.
    b) 6–8. Concerning Levites' portions.
    c) 9–22. True and false prophets.
19. Sixth commandment precepts.
    a) 1–13. Cities of refuge for homicides.
    b) 14–21. Indirect manslaughter.
20. Military laws.
    a) 1–4. Priests are to encourage the warriors.
    b) 5–9. The captain and the released soldiers.
    c) 10–20. The treatment of the enemy.
21. Capital punishment and the treatment of wives.
    a) 1–9. Unknown murder.
    b) 10–17. Treatment of wives.
    c) 18–21. Punishment of the rebellious son.
22. Kindness and marriage laws.
    a) 1–12. Ethical precepts, mostly on kindness.
    b) 13–30. Concerning fornication.
22. Citizens of the theocratic state.
    a) 1–19. Qualifications for citizenship.
    b) 20–25. Conduct and character of the true citizen.
24. Marriage laws and warnings against oppression, injustice.
    a) 1–5. Marriage laws.
    b) 6–15. Warnings against oppression.
    c) 16–22. Warnings against injustice.
25. Stripes, Levirate law, sundry precepts.
    a) 1–4. Punishment by stripes.
    b) 5–10. Levirate law.
    c) 11–12. Punishment of immodesty.
    d) 13–16. Fairness in weights and measures.
    e) 17–19. Annihilation of Amelek commanded.
26. Forms for prayer and the closing exhortation.
    a) 1–15. Formulas for prayer and sacrifice.
    b) 16–19. The closing exhortation.

PART III. THIRD ADDRESS, 27–30.

27. Invocation of blessings and curses on Gerizun and Ebal.
    a) 1–8. Order to inscribe the law at Gerizun and Ebal.
    b) 9–26. Invocation of curses or blessings for disobedience and obedience.
28. Presentation by Moses of blessings and curses.
    a) 1–14. Blessings for obedience.
    b) 15–48. Curses for disobedience.
    c) 49–68. Prediction of total destruction.
29. A call to the people to repledge themselves to the covenant.
    a) 1–9. Moses' appeal to God's past mercy.
    b) 10–15. A call for renewed pledging to the covenant.
    c) 16–29. Apostacy will bring on rejection.
30. Promised mercy and proffered choice.
    a) 1–10. Mercy to repentant captive Israel.
    b) 11–20. Proffered choice.

PART IV. CLOSE OF LIFE AND WORKS OF MOSES, 31–34.

31. Moses delivers his office and work to Joshua.
    a) 1–8. Exhortation to the people and Joshua.
    b) 9–13. Provisions for the preservation of the law.
    c) 14–23. God's charge to Moses and Joshua.
    d) 24–30. The priests as custodians of the law.

32. Moses' song of God's mercy and vengeance.
  a) 1–43. The song. [1] 1–3. Introduction.
    [2] 4–18. God's faithfulness. Israel's faithfulness.
    [3] 19–33. Divine chastisement and the need of it.
    [4] 34–43. God's compassion on his people.
  b) 44–52. Exhortations and Moses viewing Canaan.
33. Moses' parting blessings on the tribes of Israel.
  a) 1–5. Introduction : the majesty of God.
  b) 6–26. The blessings on the tribes.
  c) 27–29. Conclusion : Excellency of Israel.
34. Death and burial of Moses, 1–12.
Psalm 90. A prayer of Moses, the man of God.

7. AGE OF JOSHUA. BOOK OF JOSHUA.

PART I. DEEDS OF WAR: THE CONQUEST OF CANAAN, 1–12.

  Hurlbut, Pages 51–54.
  §1. The passage of the Jordan, 1–5.
1. The divine summons to war.
  a) 1–9. God's command to Joshua.
  b) 10–18. Joshua's command to the people.
2. The sending of the spies to Jericho.
  a) 1–7. The sending and their reception by Rahab.
  b) 8–20. Rahab's agreement with the spies.
  c) 21–24. Their return to Joshua.
3. The crossing of the Jordan.
  a) 1–8. Preparations for crossing.
  b) 9–17. The miraculous crossing.
4. Memorial at Gilgal of stones out of Jordan.
  a) 1–14. The setting up of the memorial stones.
  b) 15–24. The return of the waters of the Jordan.
5. Consecration to the holy war.
  a) 1–9. Renewal of circumcision.
  b) 10–12. Cessation of the manna.
  c) 13–15. The angel of Jehovah.
  §2. The conquest of the south, 6–10.
6. The conquest of Jericho.
  a) 1–14. Preparation for the conquest.
  b) 15–25. Capture and destruction of the city.
7. Achan's theft and punishment.
  a) 1–15. The theft and its consequences.
  b) 16–26. The discovery and punishment of it.
8. Conquest of Ai. Blessings and curses.
  a) 1–9. The divine command to attack Ai.
  b) 10–29. Its capture and destruction.
  c) 30–35. Blessings and curses at Ebal and Gerizun.
9. The trick of the Gibeonites.
  a) 1–15. Their trick.
  b) 16–27. Their preservation.
10. Victory of Gibeon and conquest of South Canaan.
  a) 1–5. Siege of Gibeon by the kings.
  b) 6–15. Battle at Gibeon.
  c) 16–27. Flight and destruction of the kings.
  d) 28–43. Conquest of the cities of the south.
  §3. Conquest of the north, 11–12.

11. Defeat of the northern kings and subjugation of the land.
    a) 1–6. The second alliance of Canaanite kings.
    b) 7–9. The victory at Merom.
    c) 10–15. Subjugation of the remaining lands.
    d) 16–23. Summary of the lands taken.
12. List of kings conquered by the Israelites.
    a) 1–6. Those conquered under Moses.
    b) 7–24. Those conquered under Joshua.

PART II. WORKS OF PEACE: POSSESSION OF CANAAN, 13–24.

§1. The division of the land among the tribes, 13–19.
Hurlbut, Pages 55–59.
13. Territory of the trans-Jordanic tribes.
    a) 1–7. The divine command to divide the land.
    b) 8–14. General boundary of trans-Jordanic possessions.
    c) 15–23. Possessions of Reuben.
    d) 24–32. Possessions of Gad and Manasseh.
14. Remarks concerning the division. Inheritance of Caleb.
    a) 1–5. Remarks on the division.
    b) 6–15. Caleb's inheritance.
15. Inheritance of the tribe of Judah.
    a) 1–12. The borders of Judah's possession.
    b) 13–20. Caleb's land in Judah. Caleb's daughter, Achsa.
    c) 21–32. Judah's cities in the south.
    d) 33–47. Judah's cities in the low lands.
    e) 48–60. Judah's cities in the mountains.
    f) 61–63. Judah's cities in the desert.
16. 1–10. The inheritance of Ephraim.
17. The inheritance of Manasseh. Complaint of Ephraim.
    a) 1–13. Inheritance of Ephraim.
    b) 14–18. Complaint of Ephraim.
18. Tabernacle at Shiloh. Inheritance of Benjamin.
    a) 1–10. Erection of the Tabernacle at Shiloh.
    b) 11–20. Territory of Benjamin.
    c) 21–28. Cities of Benjamin.
19. Inheritance of the remaining tribes viz.:
    a) 1–9. Of Simeon.
    b) 10–16. Of Zebulon.
    c) 17–23. Of Issachar.
    d) 24–31. Of Assher.
    e) 32–39. Of Naphtali.
    f) 40–48. Of Dan.
    g) 49–51. Of Joshua.

§2. Selection of cities of Refuge and Levitical towns, 20–21.
20. 1–9. Selection of cities of refuge.
21. Appointment of towns for priests and Levites.
    a) 1–8. Source and number of Levitical cities.
    b) 9–19. Priest cities.
    c) 20–45. Cities assigned to each of the families of Levi.

§3. The last days of Joshua, 22–24.
22. Return of the two and a half tribes to their land.
    a) 1–8. Their dismissal by Joshua.
    b) 9–20. Israel's complaint against their altar.
    c) 21–34. They justify themselves before a committee.

23. Joshua's first farewell address.
   a) 1-11. God's future assistance.
   b) 12-16. Warning against apostasy.
24. Joshua's second farewell address. Conclusion.
   a) 1-15. The farewell address.
   b) 16-28. Renewal of the covenant.
   c) 29-33. Death of Joshua and Eleazar.

8. AGE OF JUDGES. BOOK OF JUDGES.

Hurlbut, Pages 61-63.

PART I. HISTORICAL NARRATIVE, 1-16.

§1. From Joshua to Shaingar, 1-3.
1. Hostilities between Israelites and Canaanites.
   a) 1-21. The wars of Judah and Simeon.
   b) 22-33. State of affairs in Northern Israel.
   c) 34-36. The condition of Dan. See also Chaps. 17-18.
2. Apostasy of Israel from Jehovah.
   a) 1-10. Prediction of trouble. Death of Joshua.
   b) 11. Sinfulness of Benjamin. See Chaps. 19-21.
   c) 11-23. Apostasy and punishment of Israel.
3. Canaanites. Judges, Othniel, Ehud and Shamgar.
   a) 1-6. Israelites troubled by the Canaanites.
   b) 7-11. Cushaurishathaim and Othniel.
   c) 12-30. Eulog, the Moabite, and Ehud.
   d) 31. The Philistines and Shamgar.

§2. Deborah and Barak, 4-5.
4. Deliverance by Deborah and Barak.
   a) 1-3. Israel oppressed by Jabin.
   b) 4-16. Defeat of Jabin's captain Sisera by Deborah and Barak.
   c) 17-24. Death of Sisera at the hand of Jael.
5. Deborah's song of victory.
   a) 1-5. Praise of Jehovah.
   b) 6-9. Israel's previous disgrace.
   c) 10-12. Deborah's celebration of her deliverance.
   d) 13-18. Deborah's helpers from Israel.
   e) 19-22. The battle.
   f) 23-27. Praise of Jael's work.
   g) 28-31. The mourning for Sisera at his home.

§3. Gideon and his family, 6-9.
6. Midianite oppression and call of Gideon.
   a) 1-10. Midianite oppression.
   b) 11-24. The call of Gideon as deliverer.
   c) 25-32. Destruction of the altar of Baal by Gideon.
   d) 33-44. Collection of the army and the sign of the fleece.
7. Gideon's victory over the Midianites.
   a) 1-8. The reduction of his army.
   b) 9-18. Gideon encouraged by a dream.
   c) 19-25. Complete victory over Midian.
8. Pursuit of the foe and close of Gideon's life.
   a) 1-9. Pursuit of Midian.
   b) 10-21. Vengeance on Zebah and Zalmunna.
   c) 22-35. Refusal of the crown and close of his life.

9. Abimelech's sins and end.
    a) 1–6. Abimelech made king of Shechem.
    b) 7–21. Jotham's parable.
    c) 22–33. Conspiracy of Shechem against Abimelech.
    d) 34–49. Abimelech's war against the Shechemites.
    e) 50–57. Death of Abimelech.
    f) Story of Ruth. [See below.]
    §4. Jephthah, the Gileadite, 10–12.
10. Oppression in the north and across the Jordan.
    a) 1–2. Judge Tola, of Issachar.
    b) 3–5. Judge Jair, of Gilead.
    c) 6–18. Oppression by Ammonites.
11. Deliverance by Jephthah.
    a) 1–11. Agreement between Jephthah and the Gileadites.
    b) 12–28. Jephthah's negotiations with the Ammonites.
    c) 29–40. Jephthah's vow and victory.
12. Judgeship of Jephthah and others.
    a) 1–7. His strife with Ephraim and his judgeship.
    b) 8–15. Judges Izban, of Bethlehem; Elon, of Zebulon; Abdon, of Ephraim.
    §5. Samson's life and conflicts with the Philistines, 13–16.
13. Birth of Samson.
    a) 1–7. Time and announcement of the birth.
    b) 8–20. The angel teaching the parents the "manner of the child."
    c) 21–25. Birth and childhood of Samson.
14. Samson's first transactions with the Philistines.
    a) 1–9. Samson's courtship at Timnah.
    b) 10–20. Samson's wedding and riddle.
15. Samson's further conflicts with the Philistines.
    a) 1–8. His revenge on the Philistines.
    b) 9–20. Judah's treachery and Samson's victory over the Philistines.
16. Samson's fall and death.
    a) 1–21. Samson and Delilah.
    b) 22–31. Samson's misery and triumph in death.

PART II. APPENDIXES: STATE OF SOCIETY, 17–21.
    §1. Idolatry in Israel, 17–18.
17. Image worship in the house of Micah.
18. Removal of the image worship to Laish-Dan.
    a) 1–10. Danite spies and the priest of Micah.
    b) 11–31. The stealing of the image by Danite emigrants.
    §2. The sin and punishment of Benjamin, 19–21.
19. The horrible crime at Gibeah in Benjamin.
    a) 1–15. A Levite of Bethlehem fetching his wife home.
    b) 16–30. The outrage of the men of Gibeah.
20. Vengeance on Benjamin for connivance at the crime.
    a) 1–11. Decision of the council against Gibeah.
    b) 12–29. Unsuccessful wars against Benjamin.
    c) 30–48. Benjamin destroyed by stratagem.
21. Benjamin preserved from extinction.
    a) 1–12. Destruction of the men at Jabesh-Gilead.
    b) 13–25. Capture of the dancing girls at Shiloh.
    §3. The book of Ruth. Light amid the darkness.
1. Ruth coming with Naomi to Bethlehem, 1–22.
2. Ruth gleaning in the field of Boaz, 1–23.

3. 1–18. Ruth seeking the marriage of Boaz.
4. The marriage of Ruth and Boaz.
    a) 1–8. Levirate law.
    b) 9–19. Marriage of Ruth and Boaz.
    c) 20–22. The genealogy of Perez.

I SAMUEL: HISTORY OF SAMUEL AND SAUL.

9. AGE OF SAMUEL, THE REFORMER, 1–7.

1. Samuel's birth and infancy.
    a) 1–8. Samuel's parents.
    b) 9–20. Hannah's prayer and its answer.
    c) 21–28. Samuel's dedication to Jehovah.
2. Hannah's song and Eli's doom.
    a) 1–11. Hannah's song of victory.
    b) 12–21. Sins of Eli's sons and ministry of Samuel.
    c) 22–36. Announcement of the doom of Eli's house.
3. Call of Samuel and God's message to Eli.
    a) 1–10. The Lord's call to Samuel.
    b) 11–18. God's message to Samuel for Eli.
    c) 19–4 : 1. Samuel established as prophet.
4. God's judgment on the nation and the house of Eli.
    a) 1–11. Defeat of Israel and capture of the ark.
    b) 12–22. Fall of Eli's house.
5. 1–12. Chastisement of the Philistines.
6. The return of the ark.
    a) 1–9. The Philistines resolve to restore the ark.
    b) 10–7 : 1. The return of the ark.
7. Official life of Samuel as Judge.
    a) 2–6. National repentance and reformation.
    b) 7–12. Rout of the Philistines at Mizpeh.
    c) 13–17. Summary account of Samuel's work as Judge.

SECOND STAGE. THE MONARCHY, 1095–586.

I SAM. 8–II CHR. 36. ISA., JERE. AND MANY OF THE MINOR PROPHETS. MOST OF THE PSALMS, PROV., ECCL. AND SONG OF SOLOMON.

EPOCH I. THE UNDIVIDED MONARCHY.

10. THE REIGN OF SAUL, 40 YEARS, I Sam. 8–31.

    Hurlbut, Pages 64–67.
    §1. Appointment of the first king, 8–10.
8. The demand for a king.
    a) 1–9. The Elders' demand for a king.
    b) 10–22. The request granted under Samuel's protest.
9. Saul's first anointing by Samuel.
    a) 1–14. Saul divinely brought to Samuel.
    b) 15–27. Saul entertained by Samuel.
10. Anointing and election of Saul as king.
    a) 1–16. Anointing and confirmation by signs.
    b) 17–27. Election by lot and installation.
    §2. Saul's reign till his rejection, 11–15.
11. Establishment of Saul's kingdom.
    a) 1–11. Saul's victory over the Ammonites.
    b) 12–15. Confirmation of Saul's election at Gilgal.
12. Samuel's farewell address.
    a) 1–5. His own official integrity.
    b) 6–12. His rebuke of the people.
    c) 13–25. Warnings and encouragements for the future.

13. Saul's disobedience at Gilgal.
    a) 1–7. The revolt from the Philistines.
    b) 8–14. Saul's wilfulness and penalty.
    c) 15–23. Philistine oppression.
14. Jonathan's victory of the Philistines.
    a) 1–15. His exploits at Michmash.
    b) 16–23. Rout of the Philistines.
    c) 24–46. Saul's rash oath and its consequences.
    d) 47–52. Summary account of Saul's reign.
15. Rejection of Saul.
    a) 1–9. His commission to destroy Amelek.
    b) 10–23. The penalty of his disobedience.
    c) 24–31. The kingdom rent from Saul.
    d) 32–35. Samuel executes Agag and leaves Saul.
  §3. Decline of Saul and rise of David, 16–31.
    a) David's court life, 16–20.
16. Anointing of David and introduction to the court.
    a) 1–5. Samuel's mission to Bethlehem.
    b) 6–13. Anointing of David by Samuel.
    c) 14–23. David's introduction to the court of Saul.
17. David's victory over Goliath.
    a) 1–11. The challenges of the Philistine Goliath.
    b) 12–31. David's errand to Saul's camp.
    c) 32–54. The victory of faith, cf. Ps. 9.
    d) 55–58. Saul's inquiry about David.
18. Beginning of Saul's jealousy of David.
    a) 1–9. David's favor with Jonathan and the people.
    b) 10–16. Saul's attempt to get rid of David.
    c) 17–30. Saul's treacherous dealings with David.
19. David's flight from Saul to Samuel.
    a) 1–7. Jonathan's intercession for David.
    b) 8–17. David's escape from Saul, Ps. 59.
    c) 18–24. David's flight to Samuel at Ramah, Ps. 11, 6, 7.
20. The friendship between David and Jonathan.
    a) 1–11. David's consultation with Jonathan.
    b) 12–23. Renewal of the covenant between them.
    c) 24–34. Saul's intentions tested by Jonathan.
    d) 35-42. The parting of Jonathan and David.
    b) David's life as an outlaw, 21–31.
21. David's flight.
    a) 1–9. To Nob.
    b) 10–15, To Gath, Ps. 56.
22. David and his followers. Saul's vengeance . . . .   I Chron.
    a) 1–5. David with his followers, Pss. 34, 57, 63, 42 . .   12 : 1–19.
    b) 6–23. Saul's vengeance on the priests of Nob. Ps. 17, 35,
             52, 64, 109, 140.
23. David's rescue of Keilah and abode in Ziph, Ps. 31.
    a) 1–6. David's rescue of Keilah.
    a) 7–15. Intended treachery of the Keilites . . . . . .   I Chron.
    c) 16–28. David in the wilderness of Ziph. Ps. 54, 57,
              58, 63.
24. David at Engedi.
    a) 1–8. Sparing Saul's life.
    b) 9–15. Protesting his innocence.
    c) 16–22. Saul's momentary remorse.

25. Death of Samuel. David and Nabal.
    - a) 1. Death of Samuel.
    - b) 2–13. Nabal's churlish folly.
    - c) 14–35. Abagail's timely prudence.
    - d) 36-4. Nabal's death and Abagail's marriage.
26. Saul's fresh pursuit of David.
    - a) 1–4. Treachery of the Ziphites.
    - b) 5–12. Saul's life again spared by David.
    - c) 13–25. David's final expostulation with Saul.
27. David as a Philistine vassal (1–12). Ps. 141 . . . .   12 : 1–7
28. Muster of the Philistines. Saul and the witch, 1 -25.
29. David's dismissal from the Philistine army, 1–11 . . .   12 ; 19- 22.
30. David's vengeance on Amelek.
    - a) 1–20. The rescue of the captives.
    - b) 21–31. The distribution of the spoil.
31. The battle of Gilboa, 1–13 . . . .   10.

II. REIGN OF DAVID.

II SAMUEL : Hurlbut, Pages 67–71. . . . . . .   I Chron.

Part I. DAVID'S PROSPEROUS REIGN, 1–10.

§1. David's reign over Judah alone, 1–4.
1. David's behavior on hearing of Saul's death.
    - a) 1–16. Tidings of Saul's death brought to David.
    - b) 17–27. David's lamentation for Saul and Jonathan.
2. The rival kingdoms.
    - a) 1–7. David made king of Judah.
    - b) 8–32. The civil war.
3. Abner's revolt to David.
    - a) 1–5. The increase of David's family.
    - b) 6–16. Abner's dissatisfaction and revolt to David.
    - c) 17–27. Abner's visit to David and death.
    - d) 28–39. David's displeasure at Joab's deed of murder.
4. Murder of Ishbosheth, king of Israel.
    - a) 1–7. The murder.
    - b) 8–12. Execution of the murderers.
        §2. Rise of David's power, 5–10 . . . . . .   11–19.
        Hurlbut, Pages 72-76.
5. David king in Jerusalem. His family and victories . . . .   11 :
    - a) 1–10. David king in Jerusalem . . . .   11 : 1-9.
    - b) 11–16. David's family . . . .   14 : 1–7.
    - c) 17–25. Philistine opposition overcome . . . . . .   14 : 8–17.
6. David's care for religion.
    - a) 1–11. Removal of the ark from Kirjathjearim   13 : 1–14.
    - b) 12–23. Removal of the ark to Jerusalem . .   15 : 1–29.
        Pss. 68, 24, 132, 105, 96, 106, 101.
        The first solemn service and arrangement of worship .   16 : 1–43.
7. The promise of eternal dominion to David's house . . . . .   17 :
    - a) 1–3. David's desire to build a temple . . . . . .   1–2.
    - b) 4–17. God's gracious promise by Nathan . . . . . .   3–15.
    - c) 18–29. David's prayer and thanksgiving.
        Ps. 2, 45, 16, 118, 110 . . . .   16–27.
8. David's wars and officers of state . . . .   18 :
    - a) 1–14. His foreign conquests. Ps. 60, 108 . . . . .   1–13.
    - b) 15–18. His officers of state . . . .   14–17.
9. David's kindness to Mephibosheth, 1–13.

10. War with Ammonites the circumstances of the fall 19:
  a) 1–5. David's ambassadors insulted by the Ammonites. 1–5.
  b) 6–19. Campaigns against the Ammonites. Ps. 20, 21. 6–19.

PART II. DAVID'S CALAMITOUS REIGN, 11–24.
  §1. David's sin and repentance, 11–12.
11. David's fall.
  a) 1–13. David's adultery with Bath-sheba.
  b) 14–27. David's murder of Uriah.
12. David's repentance. Ps. 51, 32, 33, 103.
  a) 1–14. David rebuked by Nathan.
  b) 15–25. Death of Bath sheba's child and birth of Solomon.
  c) 26–31. Capture of Rabbah . . . . 20: 1–3.
  §2. David's punishment, 13–20.
13. Amnon's outrage and Absalom's vengeance.
  a) 1–22. Amnon's outrage.
  b) 23–39. Absalom's vengeance and flight.
14. Recall of Absalom.
  a) 1–24. Joab's stratagem and Absalom's return.
  b) 25–33. Absalom's readmission to the king's presence.
15. Absalom's rebellion and flight of David.
  a) 1–12. The rebellion of Absalom.
  b) 13–27. David's flight from Jerusalem. Ps. 3.
16. David's blessing and Absalom's entering Jerusalem.
  a) 1–14. Ziba's present and Shimei's cursing. Ps. 7.
  b) 15–23. Absalom enters Jerusalem. Ahithophel's counsel.
17. Hushai's counsel to Absalom. David enters Mahanaim.
  a) 1–14. Hushai's counsel to Absalom.
  b) 15–23. Hushai's message to David.
      Ps. 4, 5, 42, 43, 55, 62, 70, 71, 143, 144.
  c) 24–29. David arrives at Mahanaim pursued by Absalom.
18. Absalom defeated and slain by Joab.
  a) 1–8. The battle.
  b) 9–18. The death of Absalom.
  c) 19–33. The news brought to David. His grief.
19. The restoration of David's authority.
  a) 1–8. David reproved by Joab.
  b) 9–15. Negotiations for the king's recall.
  c) 16–43. David's return and incidents connected with it.
20. Sheba's insurrection.
  a) 1–13. Insurrection. Murder of Amasa by Joab.
  b) 14–26. End of the insurrection Officers of state.
  §3. Supplementary appendix to David's reign, 21–24. 20–29.
21. The famine and the Philistine wars.
  a) 1–14. The famine and its cause.
  b) 15–22. Heroic exploits in the Philistine wars . . . . 20: 4–8.
22. David's Psalm of thanksgiving. Ps. 18.
  a) 1–7. Invocation and cry for help.
  b) 8–16. Manifestation of Jehovah against David's foes.
  c) 17–25. Jehovah's help and David's rewarded integrity.
  d) 26–37. God's dealings with men. Praise of Jehovah.
  e) 38–51. Enemies destroyed. Dominion established. Thanks.
23. David's last words. His heroes.
  a) 1–7. David's last words.
  b) 8–39. David's heroes . . . . 11: 10–47.

24. David's sin in numbering the people.
    a) 1-9. The numbering of the people .   21: 1-8.
    b) 10-14. The choice of punishment   9-14
    c) 15-17. The plague.
    d) 18-25. The staying of the plague: The altar . .   18-27.
David's preparation for building the temple 22:
    a) David's preparation . . . .   1-5.
    b) David's charge to Solomon . . . . .   6-16.
    c) David's charge to the princes . . . . .   17-19.
The order of the Levites and their service 23:
    a) The classification of the Levites . . . .   1-5.
    b) The houses of the Levites . . . .   6-23.
    c) General regulations of the Levites . . . .   24-32.
The twenty-four classes of priests and Levites 24:
    a) The twenty-four classes of priests . . . . . .   1-19.
    b) The twenty-four classes of Levites . . . . . .   20-31.
The choristers 25:
    a) The families of song . . . .   1-8.
    b) The list of choir leaders . . . .   9-31.
The porters and the officers and judges 26:
    a) The porters . . . .   1-19.
    b) The officers and judges . . . .   20-32.
Officers of state 27:
    a) Captains of divisions . . . .   1-15.
    b) The princes of the tribes . . . .   16-24.
    c) The stewards of the royal possessions . . . .   25-31.
    d) The ministers of the court . . . . . .   32-34.
Public instructions to Solomon 28:
    a) Address of David to the people and to Solomon . . .   1-10
    b) The plan of the temple . . . .   11-21.
The last acts of David, the king 29:
    a) The contributions of the princes . . . . . .   1-9.
    b) The thanksgiving of David. Ps. 72, 91, 145 . . . .   10-19.
    c) Conclusion of the assembly . . . .   20-25.
    d) Close of David's reign . . . .   26-30.

PSALMS. BOOK I, 1-41.

1. The two characters.
    a) 1-3. The happiness of the righteous.
    b) 4-6. Character and doom of the sinner.
2. The Messiah enthroned.
    a) 1-3. Rebellion of the nations.
    b) 4-6. God's attitude toward them.
    c) 7-9. The Son enthroned.
    d) 10-12. Nations exhorted to submit.
3. A morning song of trust, 1-8.
4. An evening hymn of praise, 1-8.
5. A morning prayer for protection.
    a) 1-3. Petition for favorable hearing.
    b) 4-6. Psalmist's ground for confidence.
    c) 7-9. Prayer for guidance.
    d) 10-12. Prayer for punishment of godless.
6. The prayer of the chastened, 1-10.
7. The innocents' appeal to the just judge.
    a) 1-10. Prayer for God's intervention.
    b) 11-17. Judicial activity of God.

8. The marvelous dignity of Man, 1–9.
9. Jehovah praised for victory.
    a) 1–10. His praise as judge of the world.
    b) 11–20. His praise as helper of the needy.
10. Continuation of Psalm 9.
    a) 1–11. Picture of the insolent wicked.
    b) 12–18. Appeal to God for their destruction.
11. Jehovah a refuge in time of fear, 1–7.
12. Prayer for help from perverse neighbors, 1–8.
13. Deliverance from despair, 1–6.
14. The corruption of a godless world, 1–7.
15. The worthy citizen of Zion, 1–5.
16. "The goodly heritage," 1–11.
17. "A prayer of David" in persecution.
    a) 1–5. Appeal to God for justice.
    b) 6–12. Prayer for protection.
    c) 13–15. Prayer for help of God.
18. David's Psalm of thanksgiving.
    a) 1–6. Invocation and cry for help.
    b) 7–15. Manifestation of Jehovah against David's foes.
    c) 16–24. Jehovah's help and David's rewarded integrity.
    d) 25–36. God's providence. Praise of God.
    e) 37–50. Enemies destroyed, dominion, thanks.
19. The glory of God in work and word.
    a) 1–6. In the heavens.
    b) 7–14. In his law.
20. A prayer for the king's success, 1–9.
21. Celebration of the king's victory.
    a) 1–7. Thanks for past victory.
    b) 8–13. Anticipation of future triumphs.
22. The suffering Savior's Psalm.
    a) 1–10. His plaintive cry to God.
    b) 11–21. Prayer for deliverance.
    c) 22–26. Thanksgiving for answered prayer.
    d) 27–31. Extension of Jehovah's kingdom.
23. The shepherd Psalm.
24. The king of glory entering Zion.
    a) 1–6. The song in ascending the hill.
    b) 7–10. The song at entering the city.
25. Prayer for forgiveness and guidance.
    a) 1–7. Petition for guidance and pardon.
    b) 8–14. Character of God the ground of his prayer.
    c) 15–22. Renewed prayer for salvation.
26. David's profession of integrity, 1–12.
27. Jehovah the sure and only refuge.
    a) 1–6. The sure refuge in his pavilion.
    b) 7–14. Jehovah the only sure refuge.
28. Deliverance from the death of the wicked, 1–9.
29. The march of the thunder storm, 1–11.
30. Deliverance from the brink of ruin, 1–12.
31. The soul in anguish committed to the God of truth.
    a) 1–8. The prayer of faith.
    b) 9–18. Memory of mercies in present sorrow.
    c) 19–24. Thanksgiving for danger passed.
32. The way to the joy of sin forgiven, 1–11.

33. Joy in the Lord.
    a) 1–3. Call to praise the Lord.
    b) 4–19. Why he should be praised.
    c) 20–22. We will rejoice in him.
34. God's care over those who fear him.
    a) 1–10. God's care commended to his friends.
    b) 11–22. Instruction concerning fear of God.
35. Prayer for divine vengeance on persecutors.
    a) 1–10. Appeal to God for help.
    b) 11–18. The baseness of his persecutors.
    c) 19–28. Renewed prayer for divine interposition.
36. Human wickedness in spite of God's love.
37. The end of sinner and saint.
    a) 1–11. Warnings and counsels in temptation.
    b) 12–20. Shortlived triumph of the wicked.
    c) 21–31. God's care for the righteous.
    d) 32–40. The final contrast.
38. A sick man's penitential prayer.
    a) 1–8. Chastisement of sin.
    b) 9–14. Sufferings increased by friend and foe.
    c) 15–22. Pleadings for deliverance.
39. The nothingness of human life, 1–13.
40. Past mercies and present need.
    a) 1–11. Thanksgiving for past mercies.
    b) 12–17. Prayer for deliverance.
41. The good man deserted by his friends, 1–13.

BOOK II, 42–72.

42. The sigh of an exile.
    a) 1–5. Longing for the temple.
    b) 6–11. Confidence in God.
43. The exile's appeal to God, the judge, 1–5.
44. The sufferings of the righteous.
    a) 1–8. How God used to help his people.
    b) 9–16. Present evil condition.
    c) 17–26. Being righteous they call for help.
45. A royal wedding song.
    a) 1–9. Address to the bridegroom.
    b) 10–17. Address to the bride.
46. The Emanuel Psalm, 1–11.
47. Praises to thee, our king, 1–9.
48. The glories of Zion, the city of God.
    a) 1–8. Description of Zion.
    b) 9–14. Joy of its citizens.
49. Riches and godliness.
    a) 1–13. In this life.
    b) 14–20. In the life to come.
50. Jehovah, the righteous judge.
    a) 1–6. His coming.
    b) 7–15. His order to Israel.
    c) 16–23. His sentence on the wicked.
51. The great penitential Psalm.
    a) 1–9. Prayer for forgiveness.
    b) 10–19. Prayer for restoration.
52. The liar's fate, 1–9.
53. A variation of Psalm 14.
54. Saved by His Name, 1–7.

55. Longed-for rest from wicked men.
    a) 1-8. The Psalmist pained in view of sin.
    b) 9-16. His wrath against the wicked.
    c) 17-23. His confidence that God will requite them.
56. "What can man do unto me?" 1-13.
57. God the true refuge, 1-11.
58. Destruction of the wicked, 1-11.
59. The night watch of David's foes.
    a) 1-15. Description of his enemies.
    b) 16-17. David's trust in God.
60. A prayer for victory, 1-12.
61. The fugitive king's longing for God, 1-8.
62. "My Rock and my Salvation," 1-12.
63. Longing for God in a weary land, 1-11.
64. The fate of slanderers, 1-10.
65. A harvest Psalm, 1-13.
66. After chastisement.
    a) 1-7. Call on the nations to praise God.
    b) 8-15. Deliverance from distress.
    c) 16-20. Testimony to God's works.
67. "Let all the people praise Thee," 1-7.
68. The victorious march of God.
    a) 1-7. Invocation to sing praises to him.
    b) 8-18. Praise of God's work in the Exodus.
    c) 19-27. Praise for constant help.
    d) 28-35. Jerusalem his capital.
69. A cry for help in persecution.
    a) 1-13. Psalmist's cry in persecution.
    b) 14-21. Petition for deliverance.
    c) 22-36. Cursing his enemies.
70. A variation of Psalm 40: 13-17.
71. Joy in deliverance from foes.
    a) 1-12. Past promises pleaded in prayer for help.
    b) 13-24. Joy in the assurance of God's help.
72. The righteous king.
    a) 1-7. The nature of his rule.
    b) 8-14. Universal homage.
    c) 15-19. His kingdom a blessing.

BOOK III, 73-89.

73. The true state of the godless.
    a) 1-14. Their apparent blessings.
    b) 15-28. Their real end.
74. The desolate and helpless condition of Jerusalem.
    a) 1-11. God no more with Israel as before.
    b) 12-23. Yet there is hope that God will help.
75. God judging the proud sinners, 1-10.
76. The execution of God's sentence, 1-12.
77. Longing for God's renewed help.
    a) 1-9. Distress because of God's withdrawal.
    b) 10-20. Comfort in remembrance of God's works.
78. Lessons from Hebrew history.
    a) 1-11. The author's purpose.
    b) 12-24. God's wonders shown to his unworthy people.
    c) 25-37. The gluttons punished.
    d) 38-51. Their forgetfulness of his mercy.
    e) 52-72. Their sins and God's mercy in Canaan.

79. The ravagings of the heathen.
    a) 1–8. Sigh and complaint.
    b) 9–13. Prayer to God for help.
80. God's deserted vine.
    a) 1–7. Israel forsaken of God.
    b) 8–19. God's downtrodden vineyard.
81. Feast-day Psalm.
    a) 1–7. Call to praise God.
    b) 8–16. Israel's hardheartedness.
82. God's judgment on the gods, 1–8.
83. Prayer for help from the allied nations.
    a) 1–8. Description of the alliance.
    b) 9–18. Prayer for God's help.
84. Longing for the house of God, 1–12.
85. The exiles' longing for Canaan, 1–13.
86. Praise of God's plenteous mercy, 1–17.
87. Adoption of the nations in Zion, 1–7.
88. A cry to God from the jaws of death.
    a) 1–7. The deplorable condition.
    b) 8–10. Deserted by friends.
    c) 11–18. Appeal to God.
89. The everlasting covenant with David.
    a) 1–4. The sure mercies of David.
    b) 5–18. The glory of the Covenant God.
    c) 19–28. The anointed of God.
    d) 29–37. Faithful covenant with David's children.
    e) 38–52. Prayer on the ground of divine promises.

BOOK IV, 90–106.

90. The limits to human life.
    a) 1–4. The eternity of God.
    b) 5–10. Brevity of human life.
    c) 11–17. Prayer for mercy.
91. "My Refuge and my Fortress," 1–16.
92. A song for the Sabbath day.
    a) 1–5. Praise of God.
    b) 6–15. State of sinner and saint.
93. The Lord reigneth, 1–5.
94. The God of vengeance.
    a) 1–11. The foolish raging of the wicked.
    b) 12–23. Blessedness of abiding in God.
95. Praise to the Sovereign King.
    a) 1–6. Call to praise and worship him.
    b) 7–11. Warning from the wilderness.
96. Praise and adoration to the universal Lord, 1–13.
97. Universal joy in God's reign, 1–12.
98. Universal song of praise to God, 1–9.
99. Tersanctus, the thrice Holy One, 1–9.
100. Praise him in his courts, 1–5.
101. Godly man's triumph over evil, 1–8.
102. A prayer for the afflicted.
    a) 1–11. Complaint of his present condition.
    b) 12–22. Contemplation of the better future.
    c) 23–28. Hope in God.

103. Praise of God's works in the Kingdom of Grace.
    a) 1–5. Call on the soul to bless God.
    b) 6–18. God's boundless mercy.
    c) 19–22. The majesty of this merciful God.
104. Praise of God's works in the kingdom of nature.
    a) 1–9. On the first two days of creation.
    b) 10–18. On the third day.
    c) 19–30. On the fourth and fifth days.
    d) 31–35. The seventh-day praise.
105. Praise of God in covenant with Israel.
    a) 1–15. God's care over the patriarchs.
    b) 16–24. His care over Joseph.
    c) 25–45. Deliverance from Egypt.
106. Confession of national sins.
    a) 1–5. Call to praise God for his mercy.
    b) 6–12. Israel's sin and God's mercy in Egypt.
    c) 13–23. Sins in the wilderness.
    d) 24–33. Their sins at Kadesh and in Moab.
    e) 34–43. Their sins in Canaan.

BOOK V, 107–150.

107. Thanksgiving for answered prayers.
    a) 1–3. Introduction.
    b) 4–9. The feeding of exiles.
    c) 10–16. Deliverance of captives.
    d) 17–22. The healing of the sick.
    e) 23–32. Deliverance of the shipwrecked.
    f) 33–38. Deliverance from famine.
    g) 39–43. Deliverance from tyranny.
108. Praise and prayer (Pss. 57 and 60).
    a) 1–5. Praise for mercy (Ps. 57 : 11).
    b) 6–13. Prayer for deliverance (Ps. 60 : 5–12).
109. Some enemy cursed.
    a) 1–5. Sigh and complaint.
    b) 6–20. Prayer for God's wrath on his foe.
    c) 21–31. Prayer for God's blessing on himself.
110. The conquering king, 1–7.
111. Praise of the works and mercy of God, 1–10.
112. Blessedness of the God-fearing man, 1–10.
113. The humility of the majestic God, 1–9.
114. Song of the Exodus, 1–8.
115. Exhortation to trust in God.
    a) 1–8. Superiority of God over idols.
    b) 9–18. Therefore put your trust in him.
116. Praise of delivering mercy.
    a) 1–9. Acknowledgement of divine help.
    b) 10–19. Resolution to praise God publicly.
117. Hallelujah of the heathens, 1–2.
118. The song of the Temple dedication.
    a) 1–19. Song of the procession.
    b) 20–29. Song of the receiving Levites.
119. Contemplation of God's Word.
    a) 1–8. Blessedness of observing the Word of God.
    b) 9–16. God's word is the young man's guide.
    c) 17–24. Psalmist's purpose to observe it.
    d) 25–32. Help according to the Word.
    e) 33–40. Teach me to keep thy Word.

  f) 41–48. Prayer for the joy of knowing the Word.
  g) 49–56. Hope and comfort from the Word.
  h) 57–64. Observing the Word is his portion in life.
  i) 65–72. Affliction teaches to observe God's Word.
  j) 73–80. Affliction and comfort through it.
  k) 81–88. Prayer for this help.
  l) 89–96. Firmness and breadth of God's Word.
  m) 97–104. Word sweet because it make wise.
  n) 105–112. The Word a guide which he follows.
  o) 113–120. Hope in God's Word over against sinners.
  p) 121–128. Reliance on God's word in these evil times.
  q) 129–136. Sorrows for those unfaithful to God's Word.
  r) 137–144. Zeal for God's Word.
  s) 145–152. God help me who observe thy Word.
  t) 153–160. Observers of God's Word are saved.
  u) 161–168. God's word is joy, peace and hope in persecution.
  v) 169–176. Prayer for a hearing from God.
120. The lamb in the midst of wolves, 1–7.
121. The exiles' mountain of help, 1–8.
122. Peace be within thy walls, oh Jerusalem! 1–9.
123. Looking to the Lord for mercy, 1–4.
124. Israel's help in the Lord, 1–8.
125. The eternal mountains, 1–5.
126. The returned captives, 1–6.
127. An Gottes Segen ist alles gelegen, 1–5.
  Or God's blessings as free gift.
128. God's blessings given as reward of labor, 1–6.
129. "Cast down but not destroyed," 1–8.
130. "Out of the depth," 1–8.
131. A Psalm of humility, 1–3.
132. A place for God and the ark.
  a) 1–10. Prayer for blessings on Israel.
   11–18. God's promised help.
133. The preciousness of brotherly unity, 1–3.
134. Mutual blessings, 1–3.
135. A Bible Mosaic, 1–21.
136. His mercy endureth forever, 1–26.
137. Weaping for Zion by the rivers of Babylon, 1–9.
138. David's thanksgiving and trust, 1–8.
139. Omniscience and omnipresence of God.
  a) 1–12. Praised in reference to the Psalmist.
  b) 13–24. Praised because man is wonderfully formed.
140. Deliverance prayed for.
  a) 1–5. Description of the foes.
  b) 6–13. Reliance on God.
141. A prayer as evening incense, 1–10.
142. The prayer of an imprisoned soul, 1–7.
143. Suplications in distress.
  a) 1–6. The desolate condition.
  b) 6–12. Prayer for speedy deliverance.
144. God is the king's great help in war, 1–15.
145. The all-bountiful Provider.
  a) 1–9. Praise of his attributes.
  b) 10–21. Praise of his government.
146. Trust in God not in princes, 1–10.
147. Thanksgiving for restoration of Jerusalem, 1–20.
  a) 1–6. Call to praise God.

     b) 6–11. God's general providence.
     c) 12–20. Jerusalem called on to praise God.
148. Let all praise God for Jerusalem's establishment, 1–14.
149. God praised for his defence of Jerusalem, 1–9.
150. Doxology of praises, 1–6.

I Kings. 12. REIGN OF SOLOMON, 40 YEARS. I KINGS, 1–11. II Chr. 1-9.

 1. Anointing and accession of Solomon.
    a) 1–10. Adonijah's attempt to seize the throne.
    b) 11–31. The attempt frustrated by Nathan.
    c) 32–40. Solomon anointed king.
    d) 41–53. Adonijah pardoned by Solomon.
 2. Solomon's accession and establishment of his kingdom.
    a) 1–11. David's last instructions and death.
    b) 12–25. Adonijah forfeits his life.
    c) 26–46. Punishment of Abiathar, Joab and Shimei.
 3. Solomon's marriage, worship at Gibeon, judicial wisdom.
    a) 1–3. Solomon's marriage and religious state of the kingdom.
    b) 4–15. Solomon's sacrifice and dream at Gibeon . . . 1 : 1–13.
    c) 16–28. Solomon's judicial wisdom.
 4. Solomon's ministers of state, regal splendor and wisdom.
    a) 1–20. Solomon's ministers and officers.
    b) 21–28. Solomon's regal splendor.
    c) 29–34. Solomon's wisdom. Prov. 1–31. Song 1–8.
 5. Preparations for building the temple . . . . 2 :
    a) 1–12. Solomon's negotiations with Hyram of Tyre. . 1–16.
    b) 13–18. Tributary laborers . . . . 17 18.
 6. The building of the temple. (Hurlbut, pages 139–142.) . . . 3.
    a) 1–10. The outside of the building.
    b) 11–13. Promise of God during the building.
    c) 14–38. Internal arrangement of the temple-house and courts.
 7. Solomon's palace and temple furniture.
    a) 1–12. Erection of the royal palace.
    b) 13–22. The brazen pillars of the porch . . . . 3: 15–17.
    c) 23–39. Brazin sea and basins . . . . 4: 1–10.
    d) 40–51. Summary enumeration of other temple vessels. 4: 11–22.
 8. Dedication of the temple. Pss. 47, 97–100, 135, 136.
    a) 1–11. Removal of the ark to the temple . . . . . 5: 1–14.
    b) 12–21. Solomon's prayer at the entrance of the ark . 6: 1–11.
    c) 22–53. Solomon's dedicatory prayer . . . . 6: 12–42.
    d) 54–61. Blessing the congregation.
    e) 62–66. Sacrifices and feasts . . . . 7: 1–10.
 9. Answer to Solomon's prayer. His acts.
    a) 1–9. God's answer to Solomon's prayer . . . . 7: 11–22.
    b) 10–14. Solomon's connection with Hyram . . . . . 8: 1–6.
    c) 15–25. Solomon's tribute service and buildings . . . 8: 7–16.
    d) 26–28. Solomon's navigations . . . . 8: 17–18.
10. The glory of Solomon . . . . 9: 1–28.
    a) 1–13. The visit of the queen of Sheba . . . . . . 9: 1–12.
    b) 14–29. The wealth of Solomon . . . . . { 1: 13–17.
                         9: 13–28.
11. Solomon's polygamy, idolatry, opponents and death.
    a) 1–13. Solomon's polygamy and idolatry.
    b) 14–40. Solomon's opponents. Ecclesiastes 1–12.
    c) 41–43. Solomon's death . . . . 9: 29–31.

THE BOOK OF PROVERBS.

PART I. Introduction. Discourse on wisdom, 1-9.
1. Title and admonitions to morality.
   a) 1-9. Title and purpose of the book.
   b) 10-19. Warnings against enticements to covetousness.
   c) 20-33. Wisdom's expostulations with the foolish.
2. Rewards of those who seek wisdom.
3. A discourse on kindness and truth.
   a) 1-12. Worship of Jehovah.
   b) 13-26. Blessedness of attaining true wisdom.
   c) 27-35. Practical precepts for social life.
4. Admonitions to Godliness.
   a) 1-9. To seek wisdom.
   b) 10-19. To heed instruction and avoid wickedness.
   c) 20-27. To keep the heart and shun wrong.
5. Admonition to chastity.
   a) 1-14. To avoid the snares of the strange woman.
   b) 15-23. To regard marriage and be content with it.
6. Concerning diligence and parental instruction.
   a) 1-11. Diligence commended.
   b) 12-19. The mischievous person.
   c) 20-35. The value of parental instruction.
7. Warnings against the allurements of a bad woman.
8. Wisdom's discourse.
   a) 1-11. Appeal to the sons of men.
   b) 12-21. Her claim to be the guide in life.
   c) 22-31. Her relation to Jehovah.
   d) 32-36. Blessedness of those who hearken to her voice.
9. Wisdom's invitation to her feast.
   a) 1-6. The invitation.
   b) 7-12. The scoffer refuses, the wise accepts.
   c) 13-18. Contrast between the woman and her victim.

PART II. The first collection of Solomon's Proverbs, 10-22:16.
PART III. Two appendixes to the first collection, 22:17-24:34.
   1) The first collection of words of wise men, 22:17-24:22.
   2) The second collection of words of wise men, 24:23-34.
PART IV. The second great collection of Solomon's Proverbs, 25-29.
PART V. Appendixes to the second collection, 30-31.
   1) The words of Agur, son of Jakeh, 30.
   2) The words of King Lemuel, 31:1-9.
   3) The acrostic hymn, the virtuous women, 31:10-31.

CANTICLES OR SONGS OF SOLOMON.

PART I. 1-2:7. First meeting of the lovers.
PART II. 2:8-3:5. Their longing and seeking of each other.
PART III. 3:6-5:1. The wedding in the royal city.
PART IV. 5:2-8:4. Love's new seeking and finding.
PART V. 8:5-14. The sealing and meaning of the covenant.

KOHELETH OR ECCLESIASTES.

PART I. 1:1-11. Introduction of the speaker.
PART II. 1:12-3:22. Koheleth retraces his experience.
   a) 1:12-18. Of study.
   b) 2:1-11. Of royal mirth and pleasure.
   c) 2:12-26. Of fame.
   d) 3:1-15. Of opportunities.
   e) 3:16-22. Of courts of justice.

PART III. 4 : 1–16. Wrongs and miseries.
PART IV. 5 : 1–6 : 12. Consideration of:
    a) 5 : 1–7. Religionists.
    b) 5 : 8–13. Politicians.
    c) 5 : 14–20. Moderation.
    d) 6 : 1–12. Nothing is ours long.
PART V. 7 : 1–29. Lessons on various things.
    a) 7 : 1–10. Hopes.
    b) 7 : 11–18. Lessons from prosperity and adversity.
    c) 7 : 19–29. Man's freedom marred God's order.
PART VI. 8 : 1–9 : 10. Disproportion in the world.
    a) 8 : 1–5. Needed wisdom of courtiers.
    b) 8 : 6–15. Retirement from court to private life.
    c) 8 : 16–9 : 3. Inscrutibility of history.
    d) 9 : 4–10. Make life worth living.
PART VI. 9 : 11–10 : 20. Disproportion in life.
    a) 9 : 11–18. Time and chance rule.
    b) 10 : 1–7. Success of folly.
    c) 10 : 8–15. Failure of the reformer.
    d) 10 : 16–20. Evils of misgovernment.
PART VII. Closing reflections, 11 : 1–12 : 7.
    a) 11 : 1–6. Wisdom in charity.
    b) 11 : 7–12 : 7. The closing remarks.
PART VIII. 12 : 8–14. The epilogue.

EPOCH II. THE DUAL KINGDOM, 975–721.

I Kings 12. II, 17. II Chron. 10–28.
Judah. Israel.
Hurlbut, pages 86–90.

13. PERIOD OF THE DIVISION, 975–884.

I Kings.	*Division to Accession of Jehu*	II Chron.
12.	The secession of the ten tribes	10:
	a) 1–5. The proposal of the people	1–5.
	b) 6–12. The king's counselors.	6–11.
	c) 13–20. The king's final answer	12–19.
	d) 21–33. Establishment of Israel	11 : 1–17.
13.	God's testimony against Israel.	
	a) 1–10. Prophecy against it.	
	b) 11–32. Seduction of the prophet.	
14.	Reigns of Rehoboam and Jeroboam.	
	a) 1–20. Reign of Jeroboam.	
	b) Rehoboam's wars and concubines	11 : 18–23.
	c) 21–31. Shishak's invasion. Rehoboam's death	12 : 1–16.
15.	Reigns of Abijah and Asa. Reign of Nadab.	
	a) 1–8. Reign of Abijah	13 : 1–22.
	b) 9–12. Asa's reformation and wars	14 : 1–15.
	c) 13–15. Asa's religious reform	15 : 1–19.
	d) 16–24. Remainder of Asa's reign	16 : 1–14.
	e) 25–32. Reign of Nadab.	
16. 1–20.	Baasha, Elah, Zimri.	
16. 21–34.	Omri and Ahab.	
17.	First appearance of Elijah.	
	a) 1–7. Denounces Ahab and retires.	
	b) 8–24. Sent to the widow at Zerepta.	

18. Elijah's victory over the Baal prophets.
    a) 1–16. The meeting of Elijah and Ahab.
    b) 17–46. Victory over Baal.
19. Flight of Elijah to Horeb.
    a) 1–8. On the way to Horeb.
    b) 9–18. Elijah at Horeb.
    c) 19-21. Elisha called.
20. Ahab's double victory over Benhadad.
    a) 1–22. His first victory.
    b) 23–34. His second victory.
    c) 35–43. God's verdict on Ahab's conduct.
21. The story of Naboth and his vineyard.
    a) 1–16. Naboth murdered and robbed.
    b) 17–29. Ahab's punishment and doom.
The beginning of the reign of Jehosaphat . . . . 17 :
    a) His defence against Israel . . . . 1–9.
    b) The increase of his power . . . . 10–19.
22. Ahab's alliance with Jehosaphat, and death . . . . 18 :
    a) 1–14. The counsel of the false prophets . . . . . . 1–11.
    b) 15–28. Micaiah's prophecy . . . . 12–27.
    c) 29–40. Issue of the war and death of Ahab . . . . 28–34.
    d) 41–50. Reforms of Jehosaphat . . . . 19 : 1–11.
The success of Jehosaphat's measures . . . . 20 :
    a) The alarm and the fast . . . . 1–13.
    b) The answer and deliverance . . . . 14–23.
    c) The close of the reign . . . . 24–37.
    e) 51–53. Ahaziah's evil beginning.

II Kgs. 1. Ahaziah's sickness. His death announced by Elijah.
    a) 1–8. His sickness and embassy to Baalzebub.
    b) 9–18. His death announced by Elijah.
2. Elijah's ascension and Elisha's first miracle.
    a) 1–15. Elijah's ascension.
    b) 16–23. Elisha's first miracle.
3. The war of Joram and Jehosaphat against Moab.
4. Miracles of Elisha.
    a) 1–7. The widow's cruse of oil.
    b) 8–37. The Shunamite and her son.
    c) 38–44. His care for the sons of prophets.
5. Naaman, the Syrian leper.
    a) 1–19. The curing of Naaman.
    b) 20–27. The punishment of Gehazi.
6. Elisha's works and the Syrians.
    a) 1–7. The floating iron.
    b) 8–23. Elisha's deeds in the Syrian war.
    c) 24–33. Siege and famine of Samaria.
7. Elisha predicts the end of the famine.
8. Joram, of Judah, and Ahaziah. Works of Elisha.
    a) 1–6. Elisha helps the Shunamite.
    b) 7–15. He predicts the throne to Hazael.
    c) 16–24. Reign of Joram of Judah . . . . 21 : 1–20.
    d) 25–29. Reign of Ahaziah of Judah . . . . 22 : 1–6.

14. THE SYRIAN PERIOD, 884–840.
Accession of Jehu to that of Amaziah.

9. Jehu's anointing and conspiracy.
    a) 1–13. Anointing of Jehu.
    b) 14-28. Joram slain by Jehu.
    c) 29–37. Death of Ahaziah and Jezebel . . . 22 : 7–9.

10.   Fall of Ahab's family and Baalism.
                        a) 1–14.   Extermination of the house of Ahab.
                        b) 15–27.   Extermination of Baal prophets.
                        c) 28–36.   Reign of Jehu.
11.   Reign of Athaliah.   Coronation of Joash.
                        a) 1–3.   Tyranny of Athaliah.   Obadiah . . . .   22 : 10–12.
                        b) 4–20.   Her overthrow.   Crowning of Joash.
12.   Reign of Joash of Judah.   Reformation . . . .   24 :
13.   Jehoahaz and Joash.   Death of Elisha.
                        a) 1–9.   Reign of Jehoahaz.

          15.   RESTORATION OF ISRAEL, 840–780.
               Accession of Amaziah to End of Jeroboam II.

                        b) 10–25.   Reign of Joash.   Death of Elisha.
14.   Amaziah.   Jeroboam II.
                        a) 1–22.   Reign of Amaziah . . . .   25 :
                        b) 23–29.   Reign of Jeroboam.
             Joel.   Jonah.
15.   Reigns of Uzziah (Azariah) and Jotham.
                        a) 1–7.   Reign of Uzziah (Azariah) . . . .   26 :

          16.   THE FALL OF ISRAEL. 780–721.
                   Hurlbut, pages 91–92.

15.   b) 8–16.   Reigns of Zechariah and Shallum.
                        c) 17–31.   Reigns of Menehem, Pekahiah and Pekah.
                        d) 32–38.   Reign of Jotham . . . .   27 :
             Micah, Isaiah, 1–12.   Amos, Hosea.
16.   Reign of Ahaz . . . .   28 :
                        a) 1–9.   Idolatry of Ahaz and its results . . . .   1–8.
                        b) The captives released . . . .   9–15.
                        c) 10–20.   Idolatry and death of Ahaz . . . .   16–27.
17.   Hoshea and the fall of Samaria, Ps. 80.
                        a) 1–6.   Reign of Hoshea.
                        b) 7–23.   Cause of the fall.
                        c) 24–41.   The Samaritans and their worship.

OBADIAH :   DESTRUCTION OF EDOM AND GLORY OF ZION.

    JOEL :   JUDGMENT, REPENTENCE AND PROMISES.

    PART I.   The judgment and call to repentence, 1 : 1–2 : 17.

1.   Lamentation over destruction of Judah by locusts and drought.
           a) 1–16.   The plague of locusts.
           b) 17–20.   The severe drought.
2.   1–17.   The call to repentence.
           a) 1–11.   The terribleness of the locusts.
           b) 12–17.   The call to repentance.

    PART II.   The promises, 2 : 18–3 :

2.   18–27.   Promises of immediate and temporal blessings.
           a) 18–20.   Destruction of the locusts.
           b) 21–27.   The early and the latter rain.
2.   28–3 : 21.   Remote and spiritual blessings.
           a) 28–32.   The outpouring of the spirit.
           b) 3 : 1–21.   Destruction of hostile nations.

JONAH: THE SAVING LOVE OF GOD.
1. Deliverance of the sailors.
2. Jonah's prayer and deliverance.
3. Repentence and deliverance of Nineveh.
4. God's compassion.

AMOS: DESTRUCTION OF ISRAEL THREATENED.
PART I. Announcement of judgments of God, 1–2.
1. God's judgment against surrounding nations.
2. God's judgment against Moab, Judah and Israel.
PART II. Sermons of punishment against Israel, 3–6.
3. The certainty of the coming judgment.
4. Judgment brought on by impenitence.
5 and 6. Third sermon. Lamentation over Israel.
    a) 5: 1–17. Israel's ruin brought on by stubbornness.
    b) 5: 18–27. Woe to those trusting in false hopes.
    c) 6: 1–14. Woe to those who think God's day far off.
PART III. Visions of judgments, 7–9: 10.
7. Visions, locusts, fire and plumbline.
    a) 1–3. Of locusts.
    b) 4–6. Of fire.
    c) 7–9. Of the plumbline.
    d) 10–17. The interpretation.
8. The basket of ripe summer fruit.
9. 1–10. The broken altar.
PART IV. Promise of restoration to house of David. 9: 11–15.

HOSHEA: ISRAEL'S APOSTACY REPROVED AND FALL FORETOLD.
PART I. Prophecy in symbolic action, 1–3.
1. The first marriage with a harlot.
2. The husband's plea with his unfaithful wife.
3. The second symbolic marriage.
PART II. Sermons against Israel's sins.
4. Moral ruin of Israel in priest and people.
5. Reproof and threatened punishment.
6. Against Israel's formality.
7. Description of Israel's corruption.
8. Israel punished for the sin of calf-worship.
9. Israel to be sent into exile for their sins.
10. Their sins in spite of God's mercies.
11. Against the unthankful son called from Egypt.
12. Israel's Canaanite ways.
13. Israel's trouble.
14. Punishment and healing of the Apostacy.

MICAH: JUDGMENTS ON SAMARIA AND JERUSALEM.
PART I. The doom and hope of Samaria, 1–2.
1. The impending destruction of Samaria.
2. Its cause and the promised return.
PART II. The present wicked and the future good rule, 3–5.
3. Against the rulers, prophets and priests.
4. Prophecy of the Messianic kingdom.
    a) 1–8. The glorious future of Mt. Zion.
    b) 9–5: 1. The travail of Zion.
5. The Savior-Shepherd of Bethlehem promised.
PART III. God's controversy with his people, 6–7.
6. The trial and condemnation of the people.
7. Repentence of the people and their blessing.

ISAIAH. PART I, 1–39.

§1. The introduction: Juda reproved, 1–6.

1. The chastening opening address. Time of Ahaz.
    a) 2–9. Accusation against the unthankful nation.
    b) 10–20. Rebuke of their hollow, formal religion.
    c) 21–31. Jerusalem must be purified.
2–4. Through judgment to promise. Jotham.
    a) 2:1–5. The exalted Zion.
    b) 2:6–22. The judgment against pride.
    c) 3:1–15. The judgment against the rulers. (Ps. 82.)
    d) 3:16–4:1. The judgment against the women.
    e) 4:2–6. The purified Zion.
5. God's judgment against his abortive nation. Ahaz.
    a) 1–7. The parable song of the unthankful vineyard.
    b) 8–23. The seven woes against the people's sins.
    c) 24–30. The punishment.
6. The consecration of the prophet Isaiah.

§2. The book of the Immanuel, 7–12.

7. The sign of the Immanuel.
    a) 1–9. The historical situation and connection.
    b) 10–25. The sign with its immediate occasion.
8. 9:6. New signs of the judgment and announcement of deliverance.
    a) 1–4. Double sign of judgment against Syria and Ephraim.
    b) 5–22. Judgment against unbelief.
    c) 9:1–6. Establishment of God's kingdom.
9. 7–10:4. The impending judgments of God.
10. The humiliation of Assyria.
    a) 5–11. The pride of Assyria.
    b) 12–19. The judgment.
    c) 20–27. Comfort for Juda.
    d) 28–34. Assyrians before Jerusalem.
11. Exaltation of God's people and David's son.
    a) 1–10. The god-like Prince of Peace.
    b) 11–16. The salvation of his people.
12. Redeemed Zion's song of praise.

§3. Oracles against the nations, 13–23.

13. 14:23. Babylon threatened with destruction.
    a) 1–22. Destruction of the city.
    b) 14:1–23. Destruction of its king.
14. 24–32. Oracle against Assyria and Philistia.
15. Invasion of Moab.
16. Its subjection and troubles.
    a) 1–5. Its subjection to the son of David.
    b) 6–13. Punishment of its pride.
17. Sentence against Damascus and Israel.
    a) 1–6. Their common fate.
    b) 7–11. The cause of Israel's misfortune.
    c) 12–14. Vengeance on Israel's destroyer.
18. Oracle against Ethiopia, 1–7.
19. God's counsel concerning Egypt.
    a) 1–15. Divine visitation on Egypt.
    b) 16–25. Its salutary effect.
20. Oracle against Egypt and Ethiopia, 1–6.
21. Oracle concerning Babylon, Edom and Arabia.
    a) 1–10. On Babylon.
    b) 11–12. On Edom.
    c) 13–17. On Arabia.

22. Oracle against Jerusalem and Sebna.
    a) 1–14. Reproof of impenitent Jerusalem.
    b) 15–25. Deposition of Sebna.
23. Destruction and restoration of Tyre.
    a) 1–14. Its destruction by the Assyrians.
    b) 15–18. Its restoration.
§4. Prophecies on end of world, 24–27.
24. The judgment of the world.
25. The divine triumph.
26. The justification of the Lord.
27. Deliverance from the world powers.
§5. Prophecies concerning Zion, 28–35.
28. Precious corner-stone in Zion.
    a) 1–6. Prediction of Samaria's fall.
    b) 7–29. Punishment of Judah.
29. God's dealings with Jerusalem.
    a) 1–8. Siege and deliverance of Zion.
    b) 9–24. Its conduct toward prophecy.
30. Oracle against the Egyptian alliance.
    a) 1–8. Oracle against Egypt.
    b) 9–18. Disobedient Judah.
    c) 19–26. The purified people.
    d) 27–33. Destruction of Assyria.
31. Jehovah, not Egypt, is Israel's help, 1–9.
32. The transformed land and people, 1–20.
33. New oracle against Assyria.
    a) 1–12. Cry of distress.
    b) 13–24. Deliverance.
34. The final judgment.
    a) 1–4. For the whole world.
    b) 5–17. For Edom.
35. Redemption of God's people, 1–10.
§6. Appendix of historical extracts.
36. Sennacherib demands Jerusalem's surrender, 1–7.
37. Miraculous deliverance.
    a) 1–7. Hezekiah calmed by Isaiah.
    b) 8–13. Sennacherib's second demand.
    c) 14–20. Hezekiah's prayer.
    d) 21–38. Destruction of the Assyrian army.
38. Hezekiah's sickness, recovery and song.
    a) 1–8. His sickness and recovery.
    b) 9–20. His song of praise.
39. The Babylonian embassy to Hezekiah, 1–8.
    [For Part II, 40–66, see below.]

NAHUM: PROPHECY AGAINST NINEVEH.

1. The goodness and severity of God.
2. The fearful armies of God against Nineveh.
3. The ruin of Nineveh.

Epoch III. JUDAH ALONE, 721-587.

II Kings, 18-25. II Chron., 29-36.

II Kings.	17. AGE OF HEZEKIAH AND ISAIAH.	II Chron.
	Hurlbut, 92-94.	
18.	1-8. Beginning of Hezekiah's reign	29:
	a) Hezekiah's address	1-11.
	b) The cleansing of the temple	12:19.
	c) The reconsecration of the temple	20-30.
	d) The thank-offerings	31-36.
	Hezekiah keeping the passover	30:
	a) The preparation for the passover	1-12.
	b) The celebration of the passover	13-22.
	c) The second seven days of the festival	23-27.
	Hezekiah's reform	31:
	a) Appointment of the courses and contributions . . .	1-10.
	b) Arrangement of the chambers and officers	11-21.
18.	13-37. Sennacherib's invasion of Judah. (Isa. 36-39.) . . .	32:
	a) 13-16. Preparations to meet Sennacherib	1-8.
	b) 17-27. Rabshakeh's address to Eliakim. (Isa. 36:1-12.)	9-16.
	c) 28-37. Rabshakeh's address to the people. (Isa. 36:13-22.)	
19.	Jerusalem delivered from the Assyrians	, 17-23.
	a) 1-7. Hezekiah comforted by Isaiah. (Isa. 37:1-7.)	
	b) 8-13. Sennacherib's letter to Hezekiah. (Isa. 37:8-13.)	
	c) 14-19. Hezekiah's prayer. (Isa. 37:14-20.)	
	d) 20-37. Assyrian's destruction. (Isa. 37:21-38.)	
20.	Hezekiah's new lease of life.	
	a) 1-11. His sickness and recovery. Isa. 38.	
	b) 12-19. Babylonian embassy. Isa. 39.	
	c) 20-21. Close of Hezekiah's reign. Nahum.	

18. THE FALL OF JERUSALEM, 698-587.

21.	Reigns of Manasseh and Amon	II Chr. 33:
	a) 1-18. Reign of Manasseh. Prayer of Manasseh . .	1-20.
	b) 19-26. Reign of Amon	21-25.
22.	The beginning of Josiah's reign. (Jer. 1-10.)	34:
	a) 1-2. The good beginning of Josiah	1-7.
	b) 3-8. The repairing of the temple and finding the law .	8-18.
	c) 9-20. Reading of the law and consultation of Huldah.	19 28.
23.	The rooting out of idolatry. Habakkuk.	
	a) 1-3. The law read, covenant renewed. Zephaniah .	29-32.
	b) 4-20. Eradication of idolatry.	
23a.	The passover and close of Josiah's reign	35:
	c) 21-23. The great passover of Josiah	35:1-19.
	d) 24-30. Defeat and death of Josiah	20-27.
23b.	31-35. Reign of Jehoahaz. (Jere. 22:11, 12.)	36:1-4.
24.	1-7. Reign of Jehoiakim. (Jere. 22, 26, 27.)	5-8.
	8-17. Reign of Jehoiakin. (Jere. 22, 24, 29.)	9-10.
	18-20. Length and spirit of Zedekiah's reign	11-21.
25.	Fall of Jerusalem.	
	Jere. 32-34, 37-39, 52:1-11.	
	Jere. 25, 21, 22, 24, 32, 33, 34, 52, 39, 40.	
	a) 1-21. Siege and destruction of Jerusalem.	
	b) 22-30. Conclusion	22-23.

HABAKKUK: GOD'S WORD AGAINST THE WORLD POWERS.
1. The prophet's dialogue with God.
    a) 2-4. The prophet's complaint.
    b) 5-11. God's answer: The coming judgment.
    c) 12-17. Complaint of the prophet.
2. God's answer: The overthrow of the enemy.
3. Hymn: The church's answer to God's revelation.

ZEPHANIAH: WRATH AND PROMISE.
1. The threatened ruin.
2. a) 3:7. Admonition and exhortation.
3. b) 8-20. The promises to the faithful.

JEREMIAH.
PART I. Prophecies and history relating to Judah, 1-45.
§1. Addresses in the time of Josiah, 1-10.
1. The call of Jeremiah to prophetic office.
    a) 1-3. The superscription.
    b) 4-10. The call and installation.
    c) 11-19. Events connected with the call.
2. First address: Accusation of the faithless people.
    a) 1-13. Its unthankful faithlessness.
    b) 14-28. The grievousness of its apostacy.
    c) 29-37. The self-righteousness of the people.
3. Second address: The call to return home.
    a) 1-5. The difficulty to turn back.
    b) 6-10. The apostate sisters.
    c) 11-17. Invitation to come home.
    d) 18-25. Forgiveness after repentance.
4. 1-4. The blessed future.
4. The appearance of the northern enemy.
    a) 5-18. The description of its appearance.
    b) 19-31. Song concerning it.
5. The apostacy and decay of the people.
    a) 1-9. The accusation.
    b) 10-19. The prophetic judgment.
    c) 20-31. Renewed and increased accusation.
6. Universality of the judgment and decay.
    a) 1-8. The enemy before the capital.
    b) 9-21. The great depth of the inner decay.
    c) 22-30. Distress and the result of prophets' work.
7. Temple address: God's wrath against city and temple.
    a) 1-15. Repentance alone can save the temple from ruin.
    b) 16-28. Prophet's intercession and their formal whorship vain.
    c) 29-8:4. Their heathenish ways demand fearful expiation.
8. Temple address continued: The retribution.
    a) 4-6. They are always apostatizing.
    b) 7-12. Their wisdom is deceptive.
    c) 13-17. The avenger is near.
    d) 18-23. The prophet's pain.
9. Temple address concluded: The complaint.
    a) 1-8. The accusation.
    b) 9-15. The lamentation of the prophet.
    c) 16-21. Mourning.
    d) 22-25. True and false.
10. 1-16. Against idols.
10. 17-25. Submission to God's punishment.
§2. Addresses in time of Jehoiakim and Jehoiakin, 11-20.

11. The conspiracy against the word of God.
    a) 1–8. The prophet as herald of the law.
    b) 9–17. The opposition of the people.
    c) 18–23. The plot against Jeremiah at Anathoth.
12. The wonderful ways of God.
    a) 1–6. The prophet's complaint.
    b) 7–13. The answer of the avenging God.
    c) 14–17. The comforting outcome.
13. The judgment against the incorrigible nation.
    a) 1–14. Judgment symbolized by girdle and jugs.
    b) 15–27. A last warning call.
14 and 15. The Lord's word occasioned by coming famine.
    a) 14: 1–6. Description of the plague.
    b) 14: 7–12. God's rejection of Jeremiah's intercession.
    c) 14: 13–18. The false prophets.
    d) 14: 19–22. Renewed intercession of Jeremiah.
    e) 15: 1–9. Renewed rejection.
    f) 15: 10–21. Jeremiah's temptation and God's answer.
16–17 : 18. The Judge and the Savior.
    a) 16: 1–13. The divine ban against Judah.
    b) 16: 14–17: 4. Judgment and deliverance.
    c) 17: 5–11. False and true reliance or confidence.
    d) 17: 12–18. The confidence of the prophet.
17. 19–27. The honoring of the Sabbath.
18. The lesson from the potter and his clay.
    a) 1–12. The lesson of the potter and his clay.
    b) 13–23. The unteachable ones.
19. The breaking of the jug and its meaning.
20. The abused and lamenting prophet.
§3. Addresses in the time of Zedekiah, 21–24.
21. Introduction to 22 and 23.
    a) 1–10. The Pashhur message to Zedekiah.
    b) 11–14. House of David exhorted to righteousness.
22 and 23. Against the kings and the prophets.
    a) 22: 1–9. General introduction.
    b) 22: 10–19. Concerning Shallum, Jehoahaz and Jehoiakim.
    c) 22: 20–30. Oracles against Jehoiakim.
    d) 23: 1–8. The good rule of the future king.
    e) 23: 9–22. The false prophets of Jerusalem.
    f) 23: 23–32. The dream and prediction.
    g) 23: 33–40. Against the use of " Burden of the Lord."
24. The two baskets of figs.
§4. Special prophecies of the overthrow, 25–29.
25. God's judgment against the nations.
    a) 1–14. The seventy years of Babylonian captivity.
    b) 15–29. Judgment against the heathens.
    c) 30–38. Judgment against the world.
26. Judicial persecution of Jeremiah.
    a) 1–6. Introduction : The offensive address.
    b) 7–19. The judicial proceedings against him.
    c) 20–24. Death of the prophet Uriah.
27. Submission to the Babylonian yoke.
    a) 1–11. The sending of the yokes by the foreign messengers.
    b) 12–22. Warning against Zedekiah and the priests.
28. Jeremiah and Hananiah in conflict.
    a) 1–11. Hananiah's oracle and symbolic action.
    b) 12–17. Jeremiah's answer.

29. Letters to Babylon.
    a) 1–23. The first: Instruction to the exiles.
    b) 24–32. The second: Oracle over Shemiah.
        §5. Book of comfort, 30–33.
30. The deliverance of total Israel.
    a) 1–3. The theme of 30 and 31.
    b) 4–22. The deliverance of Israel.
31. Salvation and renewal.
    a) 1–22. Ephraim's share in the salvation.
    b) 23–26. Judah's share.
    c) 27–40. The entire renewal.
32. The purchase of the field at Anathoth.
    a) 1–15. The transaction.
    b) 16–25. A prayer for enlightenment.
    c) 26–44. The divine illumination.
33. Address of comfort from tenth year of Zedekiah.
    a) 1–13. Comforting of the unfortunate people.
    b) 14–26. The justified congregation of the last days.
        §6. Short utterances in time of Jehoiakim and Zedekiah, 34–39.
34. Sins of Israel.
    a) 1–7. The lot of Zedekiah.
    b) 8–22. Israel's sin against its slaves.
35. The example of the Rechabites against Judah.
    a) 1–11. The proved obedience of the Rechabites.
    b) 12–19. The sentence of God to Israel and the Rechabites.
36. Jeremiah's book of predictions and its fate.
    a) 1–8. The preparation of the book.
    b) 9–26. Its destruction by the king Jehoiakim.
    c) 27–32. Renewal of the book and oracle against the king.
37. Imprisonment of Jeremiah.
    a) 1–10. Oracle at Zedekiah's request.
    b) 11–16. Imprisonment of Jeremiah.
    c) 17–21. Interview between Jeremiah and the king.
38. New attack on the prophet's life.
    a) 1–6. Jeremiah in the hands of the hostile princes.
    b) 7–13. His deliverance through Ebedmelech.
    c) 14–28. His secret interview with Zedekiah.
39. Jeremiah at the fall of Jerusalem.
    a) 1–14. Jeremiah freed from prison.
    b) 15–18. Promise to Ebedmelech, the Ethiopian.
        §7. The prophet's work after the fall, 40–45.
40. The liberation of Jeremiah. Assembly of the people.
    a) 1–6. Liberation of the prophet.
    b) 7–16. Assembly of the people under Gedaliah.
41. Murder of Gedaliah and its consequences.
    a) 1–9. The murders.
    b) 10–18. The consequences.
42. Consultation on emigrating to Egypt.
    a) 1–16. The prophet consulted.
    b) 17–22. His unfavorable answer.
43. The flight to and sojourn in Egypt.
    a) 1–7. Emigration to Egypt.
    b) 8–13. Jeremiah in Tahpanhes (Nebuchadnezzar).
44. The last testimony against the Jews' idolatry.
    a) 1–14. Jews exhorted to keep from idolatry.
    b) 15–19. Reply of the people.
    c) 20–30. Prophet's answer.

45. Comfort and promise to Baruch.
PART II. Phrophecies against the nations, 46–52.
46. Oracles against Egypt.
    a) 1–12. Camp of Egypt on the Euphrates.
    b) 13–28. Prediction of Nebuchadnezzar's invasion.
47. Oracle against the Philistines.
48. Oracles concerning Moab.
    a) 1–25. Description of the judgment against Moab.
    b) 26–42. The cause of the judgment.
49. Oracles against surrounding nations.
    a) 1–6. Ammon. Reproof of,
    b) 7–22. Edom. Reproof of,
    c) 23–27. Damascus and Syria.
    d) 28–33. Arabian tribes threatened.
    e) 34–39. Elam.
50. Against Babylon.
    a) 1–20. Israel freed thro. destruction of Babylon by Medes.
    b) 21–32. Utter destruction of Babylon.
    c) 33–46. Israel free, Babylon ruined.
51. Oracle against Babylon continued.
    a) 1–19. Destruction of Babylon.
    b) 20–58. The destroyer destroyed.
    c) 59–64. The disposal of Jeremiah's prophecy.
52. Appendix: The destruction of Jerusalem.

LAMENTATIONS OF JEREMIAH.

1. Zion's wail over fall of Jerusalem and Judah.
2. The poet's lamentation over fall of Zion.
3. Israel's day of hope in the night of suffering.
4. Pictures of Zion's guilt and punishment.
5. The misery and hope of the captives.

THIRD STAGE: HEIROCRACY OR RULE OF PRIESTS.

EPOCH I. CLOSE OF OLD TESTAMENT HISTORY, 587–400.

19. THE BABYLONIAN CAPTIVITY, 587–536.

Hurlbut, pages 91–96.

EZEKIEL.

PART I. Before the siege. Judgment, 1–24.
    § 1. The call and first work, 1–7.
1. The vision of the glory of Jehovah.
    a) 1–4. Introduction.
    b) 5–14. The four living creatures.
    c) 15–21. The wonderful wheels.
    d) 22–28. The enthroned Jehovah.
2. Ezekiel's mission to his stiff-necked people.
    a) 1–8. His mission.
    b) 9–3:3. The roll of his prophecy.
3. Divine instruction for his work.
    a) 4–11. Divine encouragement.
    b) 12–15. Induction into office.
    c) 16–27. Instruction as to his duty.
4. Three signs of the siege of Jerusalem.
    a) 1–3. The miniature siege.
    b) 4–8. His typic actions.
    c) 9–17. The hardness of the siege.

5. The sign of the hair.
   a) 1-4. The sign.
   b) 5-17. Divine interpretation of it.
6. Prophecy against the mountains of Palestine.
   a) 1-10. Israel's ruin announced to the mountains.
   b) 11-14. Sins of people the cause of ruin.
7. Israel's desolation.
   a) 1-15. Final desolation.
   b) 16-20. Desolation of the escaped.
   c) 21-27. Sin as cause.
   §2. Concerning expulsion. Sixth year. 8-19.
8. Vision of abomination in the temple.
   a) 1-4. The introduction.
   b) 5-13. Image of jealousy and the image chamber.
   c) 14-18. Tammuz mourner and sun worship.
9. Vision of the judgment on the guilty, 1-11.
10. Vision of the coals of fire on the city.
    a) 1-7. The coals from between the wheels.
    b) 8-22. Description of the vision.
11. The vision of the leaders of the people.
    a) 1-13. The sins of the leaders reproved.
    b) 14-24. God's purpose in the punishment.
12. Signs and warning regarding the exile.
    a) 1-16. The symbolical moving.
    b) 17-20. Bread and water sign.
    c) 21-28. Repeated announcement of destruction.
13. False prophets and prophetesses.
    a) 1-16. Character and punishment of prophets.
    b) 17-23. The character and punishment of prophetesses.
14. Idolatrous seekers after oracles.
    a) 1-11. Address to oracle seekers.
    b) 12-23. God's sentence of destruction.
15. Parable of the vine for burning, 1-8.
16. Story of the lewd adulteress.
    a) 1-14. God's mercy to her in wretched infamy.
    b) 15-34. The abominable faithlessness.
    c) 35-52. The punishment.
    d) 53-63. The return of mercy.
17. The riddle about the house of David.
    a) 1-10. The riddle.
    b) 11-21. The explanation.
    c) 22-24. The prophecy.
18. The laws of divine justice.
    a) 1-9. The principle and application to the just man.
    b) 10-20. Applied to unjust and just son.
    c) 21-32. God's mercy and call to repentance.
19. Lamentation over kings of Israel.
    a) 1-9. Address to the kings.
    b) 10-14. The queen mother.
    §3. Against idolatry. Seventh year, 20-23,24.
20. Review of God's dealings with Israel.
    a) 1-9. Occasion and dealings in Egypt.
    b) 10-24. Israel in the desert.
    c) 25-31. Israel in Canaan.
    d) 32-44. Coming punishment and mercy.

21. The approaching judgment.
    a) 20:45–21:7. Picture of forest and sign of sighing.
    b) 21:8–17. Carnival of the sword.
    c) 18–22. Babylon against Israel and Ammon.
22. Jerusalem's ripeness for judgment.
    a) 1–16. Her abominations.
    b) 17–32. Burning away the dross.
    c) 23–31. General ripeness for judgment.
23. Judah's and Israel's ripeness for judgment.
    a) 1–4. Introduction.
    b) 5–10. Oholah's (Samaria's) adultery.
    c) 11–21. Oholibah's (Jerusalem's) guilt.
    d) 22–36. Oholibah's (Jerusalem's) punishment.
    e) 36–49. The abomination of the sisters.
24. Capture of Jerusalem. Ninth year.
    a) 1–14. Capture of Jerusalem and sign of the boiling pot.
    b) 15–27. Prophet's silence as sign of calamity.

PART II. During the siege. Transition, 25–32.

25. Judgment against southern nations.
    a) 1–7. Against the Ammonites.
    b) 8–11. Against the Moabites.
    c) 12–14. Against the Edomites.
    d) 15–17. Against the Philistines.
26. The fall of Tyre.
    a) 1–14. Her exile through Nebuchadnezzar.
    b) 15–21. The astonishment at her fall.
27. The glory and ruin of Tyre.
    a) 1–25. Her glory.
    b) 26–36. Her irrecoverable fall.
28. Against Tyre's princes and Sidon.
    a) 1–10. Prophecy against prince of Tyre.
    b) 11–19. Lamentation over king of Tyre.
    c) 20–26. Prophecy against Sidon.
29. Introduction to prophecy against Egypt.
    a) 1–16. General survey of the prediction.
    b) 17–21. The purpose of Egypt's ruin.
30. Prediction against Egypt.
    a) 1–19. The day of judgment.
    b) 20–26. Pharoah and the king of Babylon.
31. Egypt and Assyria.
    a) 1–9. Glory of Assyria.
    b) 10–16. Fall of Assyria.
    c) 17, 18. The lesson for Egypt.
32. The fall of Egypt.
    a) 1–16. Lamentations over Egypt.
    b) 17–32. Dirge over Egypt.

PART III. After the seige, Mercy, 33–48.
    §1. Divine promises. 33–39.

33. Renewal of Ezekiel's call.
    a) 1–20. The duty of a watchman.
    b) 21–33. The duty in respect to the capture of Jerusalem.
34. The false and the true shepherd.
    a) 1–10. The shepherds of Israel.
    b) 11–22. Jehovah's shepherd-mercy on Israel.
    c) 23–31. The true shepherd.
35. Denunciation of Edom.
    a) 1–9. Edom's mortal hatred of Israel.
    b) 10–15. Edom's greed against Israel.

36. Israel comforted.
    a) 1–15. The mountains of Israel.
    b) 16–21. Israel's profanation of God's name.
    c) 22–38. God sanctifies his name.
37. Restoration and reunion of Israel.
    a) 1–14. Resurrection of the dry bones.
    b) 15–28. Israel's reunion symbolized by two sticks.
38, 39. Against Gog of Magog.
    a) 38 : 1–13. The army and malice of God.
    b) 38 : 14–23. God's judgment against him.
    c) 39 : 1–16. Gog's defeat. Israel's victory.
    d) 39 : 17–29. Feast of God. Israel's divine favor.
    ₿2. The New Jerusalem. 40–48.
40. Description of the Temple wall courts.
    a) 1–16. The Temple wall described.
    b) 17–27. The outer court and its gates.
    c) 28–37. The inner courts and its gates.
    d) 38–49. Arrangements of inner court. The porch.
41. Description of the Temple proper.
    a) 1–14. Temple measurements.
    b) 15–26. Summary.
42. The chambers of the priests.
    a) 1–14. Sacred chambers of priests.
    b) 15–20. Dimensions of the sanctuary.
43. Entrance of God's glory. The altar.
    a) 1–12. The entrance of God's glory.
    b) 13–27. Altar of burnt offerings.
44. The service in the new Temple.
    a) 1–3. The gate of the princes.
    b) 4–16. The priests.
    c) 17–31. Priests' duties and privileges.
45. Distribution of the land.
    a) 1–9. The portion for the sanctuary, prince and city.
    b) 10–25. Israel's life and worship.
46. Ordinances for worship.
    a) 1–15. Ordinances of prince and people.
    b) 16–18. Inheritance of princes.
    c) 19–24. The courts for boiling and baking.
47. The Holy Land.
    a) 1–12. The waters of life.
    b) 13–23. The boundaries of the Holy Land.
48. Division of the land. The holy city.
    a) 1–7. The seven northern tribes.
    b) 8–22. The portion of the santuary.
    c) 23–29. The five southern tribes.
    d) 30–35. Dimensions and gates of the city.

HISTORY OF SUSANNA. (Apoch.)

a) 1–12. The lustful elders.
b) 13–27. The attempted rape.
c) 28–44. Her trial and condemnation.
d) 45–64. Her deliverance by Daniel.

DANIEL.

PART I. History, 1-6.
1. Daniel's early history.
    a) 1-7. Daniel and his companions chosen.
    b) 8-16. Daniel refuses the king's food.
    c) 17-21. Their superiority.
2. Nebuchadnezzar's dream: the four kingdoms.
    a) 1-16. The Chaldeans' failure to reveal the dream.
    b) 17-24. The dream divinely revealed to Daniel.
    c) 25-35. Daniel reveals the dream to the king.
    d) 36-45. The interpretation of the dream.
    e) 46-49. God glorified and Daniel honored.
3. Deliverance of Shadrach, Meshach and Abednego.
    a) 1-7. The command to worship the image.
    b) 8-23. The three Jews cast in the fire.
    c) 24. The prayer of the childen. (Apoch.*)
    d) 19-30. The deliverance from the fiery furnace.
4. Nebuchadnezzar's dream, a proclamation.
    a) 1-7. The proclamation and dream.
    b) 8-18. The dream told to Daniel.
    c) 19-27. The interpretation by Daniel.
    d) 28-37. The king's disease and restoration.
5. Belshazzar and the mysterious hand-writing.
    a) 1-12. The writing during the feast.
    b) 13-31. Daniel's interpretation.
6. Daniel cast in the lions' den.
    a) 1-9. The king's interdict.
    b) 10-17. Daniel cast in the den.
    c) 18-24. Daniel saved and his foes punished.
    d) 25-28. God glorified.
PART II. Visions.
7. Vision of the four kingdoms.
    a) 1-8. Vision of the four beasts.
    b) 9-14. Vision of the Messianic kingdom.
    c) 15-28. The interpretation of the visions.
8. Vision of the two world-kingdoms and their fall.
    a) 1-14. The vision of the ram and the goat.
    b) 15-27. Gabriel's interpretation.
9. The seventy weeks.
    a) 1-19. Daniel's prayer for restoration of Jerusalem.
    b) 20-27. The prophecy of the seventy weeks.
10. The appearance of a vision.
    a) 1-9. Vision of a man appears to Daniel fasting.
    b) 10-21. Michael comforts him.
11. The conflicts of the nations.
    a) 1-20. Antiochus the Great (?).
    b) 21-45. Antiochus Epiphanes (?).
13. Prophecy of the end.

BEL AND THE DRAGON. (Apoch.)

a) 1-22. Bel and his priests destroyed.
b) 23-27. Destruction of the dragon.
c) 28-42. Plots laid against Daniel.

---
*(a) 1-22. Prayer for deliverance.
(b) 23-27. Deliverance.
(c) 28-68. Their thankfulness.

Isaiah, Part II, 40–66. (Written in time of Hezekiah.)
§1. God's preparations for salvation of Israel.
40. Zion comforted.
    a) 1–11. The heralds of God.
    b) 12–26. Incomparability of God.
    c) 27–31. Israel's consequent comfort.
41. Jehovah the God of history and of prophecy.
    a) 1–7. His superiority over idols in history.
    b) 8–20. He gives his people victory.
    c) 21–29. *He* is God of prophecy.
42. The servant of God.
    a) 1–9. The servant in whom Jehovah delights.
    b) 10–17. Song of praise for deliverance.
    c) 18–25. Israel the disobedient servant.
43. Saved by grace alone.
    a) 1–7. Salvation assured.
    b) 8–13. The only true God.
    c) 14–20. The coming salvation.
    d) 21–28. Grace the motive.
44. Israel's God against idols.
    a) 6–20. Folly of idol worship.
    b) 21–28. God the only creator and redeemer.
45. Cyrus, God's anointed deliverer.
    a) 1–7. Cyrus sent forth by God.
    b) 8–17. God commands all to obey him.
    c) 18–25. God is superior to the idols.
46. Babylon's gods shall fall.
    a) 1–2. Their fall.
    b) 3–7. Their helplessness.
    c) 8–13. God alone can deliver.
47. The fall of Babylon.
    a) 1–7. Its humiliation.
    b) 8–15. Its pride and certain doom.
48. The command to escape from Babylon.
    a) 1–11. They are to be saved for God's own sake.
    b) 12–22. Urged to obey him and flee.
§2. The servant of Jehovah, 49–57.
49. The servant and Zion.
    a) 1–13. Exaltation of the servant.
    b) 14–26. The blessing of Zion.
50. Relation of Zion and the servant to God.
    a) 1–3. Zion is not divorced from God.
    b) 4–9. The servant faithful in spite of shame.
    c) 10–11. Call on the faithless to obey God.
51. Deliverance is coming.
    a) 1–8. Exhortation to trust God's promise.
    b) 9–16. Delivered by God's outstretched arm.
    c) 17–23. Afflicted Zion shall be delivered.
52. 1–12. The returning Zion.
    a) 1–6. Awake, Zion; put on thy glory.
    b) 7–12. The advent of Jehovah.
53. The suffering Saviour.
    a) 52:13-53:3. Description of the servant.
    b) 4–12. His vicarious suffering.
54. Zion, present and future.
    a) 1–10. Now barren, shall have many children.
    b) 11–17. Now tossed, shall be firmly grounded.

55. The gracious invitation.
    a) 1-5. The blessings for all.
    b) 6-13. God's mercies higher and surer than the heavens.
56. 1-8. No disqualifications for the New Kingdom.
57. Reproof of delinquents.
    a) 56:9-12. Delinquent rulers.
    b) 57:1-13. Delinquent people.
    c) 14-21. Promises to the penitent.
        §3. Completion of salvation, 58-66.
58. The reward of true righteousness.
    a) 1-5. The false worship.
    b) 6-7. The true worship.
    c) 8-14. The reward of the true.
59. Israel's sin the cause of evil.
    a) 1-8. Total depravity of Israel.
    b) 9-15. Their confession.
    c) 16-21. Deliverance coming.
60. Glorified Zion, the light of the world.
    a) 1-3. God's sun of grace arises.
    b) 4-16. Submission of the nations.
    c) 17-22. Description of the glorified city.
61. The great herald of redemption, 1-10.
62. The approaching deliverance, 1-12.
63:1-6. Judgment in Edom.
63:7-64. The longing prayer.
    a) 63:7-14. Review of past mercy.
    b) 63:15-19. Prayer for present grace.
    c) 64:1-11. Wish and prayer for grace.
65. The Lord's answer.
    a) 1-7. The source of estrangement from God.
    b) 8-12. Only a remnant saved.
    c) 13-25. Blessedness of the elect.
66. The New Jerusalem.
    a) 1-4. The spiritual worship.
    b) 5-9. Zion's blessed condition.
    c) 10-14. End of her foes.

TOBIT. (Apoch.)

1. Tobit's early life and persecution.
    a) 1-9. His life in Palestine.
    b) 10-22. His persecution for burying Jews.
2. His restoration and misfortune.
    a) 1-8. Return to his kind deeds after return.
    b) 9-14. His blindness and support.
3. Tobit's and Sara's prayers.
    a) 1-6. The reproached Tobit's prayer.
    b) 7-15. Sara's prayer on account of false accusation.
    c) 16-17. Raphael sent to heal both.
4. Tobit's charge to his son Tobias.
    a) 1-3:20-21. The loan to Gabaelus.
    b) 4-19. Fatherly advice to his son.
5. Raphael's offer to go with Tobias to Rages in Media.
    a) 1-9. Tobias finds Raphael to be an angel.
    b) 10-16. Agreement and departure.
    c) 17-22. Anna's grief at her son's departure.

6. The journey to Ecbatana.
    a) 1-8. The killing of the fish in the Tigris.
    b) 9-17. Raphael's talk about Sara.
7. The marriage of Tobias and Sara.
    a) 1-8. Their reception by Raguel.
    b) 9-18. Sara given to Tobias for wife.
8. The happy outcome of the marriage.
    a) 1-9. The demon banished. Prayer.
    b) 10-21. Raguel's thanksgiving.
9. The loan recovered by Raphael, 1-6.
10. Tobias' return with his wife to Nineveh.
    a) 1-7. Tobit's and Anna's grief for their son.
    b) 7a-12. Tobias' return home with his wife.
11. Reception and Tobit restored.
    a) 1-6. Raphael and Tobias announce the arrival.
    b) 7-16. Tobit restored to sight.
    c) 17-19. Sara heartily welcomed.
12. Raphael's advice and departure.
    a) 1-5. Their desire to pay Raphael.
    b) 6-15. Raphael's advice to be godly.
    c) 16-22. Raphael's revelation of himself.
13. Tobit's Psalm of thanksgiving.
    a) 1-7. Personal praise and confession.
    b) 8-18. Praise of Jerusalem.
14. The conclusion.
    a) 1-11. Tobit's prophecy and charge to his son.
    b) 12-15. Tobias' removal to Ecbatana.

JUDITH. (Apoch.)

1. Nabuchodonosor's victory over Arphoxad.
    a) 1-6. Nabuchodonosor's allies.
    b) 7-12. Nations who despised him.
    c) 13-16. Defeat of Arphoxad.
2. Preparation for Nabuchodonosor's revenge.
    a) 1-4. Consultation at the court.
    b) 5-13. Olophernes commissioned to prepare.
    c) 14-28. Olophernes' devastation of the west.
3. Holophernes entreated for peace, still devastates, 1-10.
4. Jews' anxiety for Jerusalem.
    a) 1-8. Their fear and Joacim's request to ward off.
    b) 9-15. Prayer and fasting in Israel.
5. Olophernes' consultation for battle with the Jews.
    a) 1-5. His anger at the Jews' opposition.
    b) 5-21. Achior's account of the Jews.
    c) 22-24. His chief men advise to fight the Jews.
6. Rejection of Ochior and his counsel.
    a) 1-9. Olophernes' contempt of the true God.
    b) 10-21. Ochior delivered to the Jews.
7. The siege of Betulua.
    a) 1-7. Preparation for attack.
    b) 8-15. Edom and Moab suggest siege.
    c) 16-22. Olophernes sets siege against it.
    d) 23-32. The distress and complaint of Betulua.
8. Deliverance promised by Judith.
    a) 1-10. Description and history of Judith.
    b) 11-27. Judith's exhortation to Ozias.
    c) 28-36. Her promise of help.

9. Judith's prayer to God.
    a) 1–6. God's past deliverance.
    b) 7–14. Prayer for help from this foe.
10. Judith's approach to the king.
    a) 1–10. Her departure from Betula.
    b) 11–23. Her introduction to the king.
11. Judith's false speech to Olophernes.
    a) 1–4, 20–23. Olophernes comforts Judith.
    b) 5–19. Her speech to him.
12. Judith's feasting with Olophernes.
    a) 1–9. Her first three days in his tent.
    b) 10–20. The private banquet on the fourth day.
13. Decapitation of Olophernes.
    a) 1–10. Olophernes slain by Judith.
    b) 11–20. The announcement to the people.
14. Judith's counsel to the townsmen.
    a) 1–4. Her counsel to show fight.
    b) 5–10. The revelation to Achior.
    c) 11–19. The discovery in Assyrian camp.
15. The joyful deliverance.
    a) 1–7. Rout of the Assyrians.
    b) 8–13. The deliverer blessed.
16. Judith's triumph and honor.
    a) 1–17. The triumphal song of Judith.
    b) 18–25. Her honored after-life.

20. THE PERSIAN PERIOD, 536–333.
EZRA, OR FIRST RETURN OF EXILES.

PART I. Return of the Jews and restoration of temple, 1–6.
1. Departure from Babylon.
    a) 1–4. Edict of Cyrus. Ps. 126, 85, 111–114.
    b) 5–6. Departure from Babylon.
    c) 7–11. Restitution of the sacred vessels.
2. List of those returning.
    a) 1–35. List of houses and families . . . . Neh. 7: 8–38.
    b) 36–39. List of the priests . . . . "   7: 39–42.
    c) 40–58. Levites, Nethenim, Servants . . . . "   7: 43–60.
    d) 61–63. Unregistered priests . . . . "   7: 63–65.
    e) 64–70. Sum total and contributions . . . . . . "   7: 66–73.
3. Restoration of the temple begun.
    a) 1–7. The altar and the sacrifices.
    b) 8–13. The foundation of temple laid. Ps. 84, 66.
4. Temple building hindered. Jews accused.
    a) 1–5. The temple building hindered. Ps. 129.
    b) 6–23. Complaints against the Jews.
5. Building of temple continued. Ps. 139.
    a) 1–5. The building begun again.
    b) 6–17. Copy of letter sent to the king.
6. The building of the temple completed.
    a) 1–12. The decree of Darius.
    b) 13–18. Completion of temple. Ps. 48, 81, 146–150.
    c) 19–22. The feast of passover.

PART II. Ezra's return and work, 7–10.
7. Ezra's return and commission.
    a) 1–10. Ezra and his companions.
    b) 11–26. Copy of his royal commission.
    c) 27–28. Ezra's thanksgiving.

8. List of houses and account of journey.
    a) 1-14. List of heads who returned. I Esdras 8: 28-40.
    b) 15-36. Account of the journey.
9. The people's sin of intermarriage.
    a) 1-4. Ezra informed of the sin.
    b) 5-15. Ezra's prayer and confession.
10. Removal of the strange wives.
    a) 1-6. Resolution to put them away.
    b) 7-17. Resolution carried out.
    c) 18-44. List of men who had strange wives.

HAGGAI: PROPHECIES URGING THE BUILDING OF THE TEMPLE.

1. The first prophecy. Neglect reproached, 1-15.
2. Three other prophecies.
    a) 1-9. Counteracting the disparagements.
    b) 10-19. How prayers will be answered.
    c) 20-23. Support and protection promised Zerubbabel.

ZECHARIAH.

PART I. Visions, 1-6.
1. Introduction and first and second visions.
    a) 1-6. Introductory summons to repentance.
    b) 7-17. First vision: the horseman among the myrtles.
    c) 18-21. Second vision: the four horns and four carpenters.
2. Third vision: the surveyor forbidden to measure, 1-13.
3. Fourth vision: Joshua, the high priest, accepted, 1-10.
4. Fifth vision: the golden candlestick, 1-14.
5. Sixth and seventh visions: the roll and the woman.
    a) 1-4. Sixth vision: the flying roll.
    b) 5-11. Seventh vision: the woman in the ephah.
6. Eighth vision and crowning of Joshua.
    a) 1-8. Eighth vision: the four war chariots.
    b) 9-15. The crowning of Joshua.
PART II. The decision regarding fast days, 7-8.
7. Obedience and disobedience.
    a) 1-3. Introduction to chapters, 7-8.
    b) 4-7. Obedience better than fasting.
    c) 8-14. Disobedience root of past misery.
8. The promised blessings.
    a) 1-17. Their joy in proportion to sorrow.
    b) 18-23. Fasts are to be turned to feasts.
PART III. Israel's security and triumph, 9-11.
9. Zion's prosperity in surrounding ruin.
    a) 1-8. Her old foes humbled.
    b) 9-17. Reign of peace in Zion.
10. God is with his people.
    a) 1-7. God the source of all.
    b) 8-12. Restoration of God's people.
11. The good shepherd rejected, 1-14.
PART IV. Israel's final victory, 12-14.
12. Siege of Jerusalem.
    a) 1-9. Jerusalem besieged and delivered.
    b) 10-14. The national mourning.
13: 1. The fountain and the shepherd.
    a) 1-6. The cleansing of the nation.
    b) 7-9. The smitten shepherd.

14. The day of the Lord.
    a) 1–5. The day of the Lord comes.
    b) 6–11. Description of the day.
    c) 12–21. Punishment of foes.

ESTHER: DELIVERANCE OF THE JEWS.

1. The divorce of Queen Vashti.
    a) 1–8. The banquet of Xerxes.
    b) 9–15. Vashti's disobedience.
    c) 16–22. Her divorce.
2. Esther's elevation. Mordecai's service.
    a) 1–4. A new Queen to be selected.
    b) 5–20. Esther chosen.
    c) 21–23. Mordecai's service.
3. Haman's design against the Jews.
    a) 1–6. His elevation.
    b) 7–15. His plot against the Jews.
4. Consultation of Mordecai with Esther.
    a) 1–3. Mordecai's mourning.
    b) 4–8. Esther charged to interfere.
    c) 9–17. Esther resolves to attempt.
5. Esther's banquet for the King and Haman
    a) 1–8. Esther's gracious reception by Xerxes.
    b) 9–14. Haman's rage against Mordecai.
6. Mordecai elevated. Haman disgraced, 1–14.
7. Haman's downfall and ruin, 1–10.
8. Mordecai advanced and counter edict.
    a) 1–2. Mordecai's advancement.
    b) 3–14. Counter edict.
    c) 15–17. Joy of the Jews.
9. Origin of Feast of Purim.
    a) 1–19. Jews avenged of their foes.
    b) 20–32. Institution of Purim.
10. Power and greatness of Mordecai.
    a) 1–3. His exaltation.
    [b 4–13. The fulfilment of his dream. (Apocrypha.)
11. His dream of the fountain and the dragons.
    a) 1–5. Stock and quality of Mordocheus.
    b) 6–12. Dream of fountain and dragons.
12. Mordocheus saves the King's life, 1–6.
13. Attempt to kill the Jews.
    a) 1–7. Copy of the King's decree of destruction.
    b) 8–18. Mordocheus' prayer for Israel.
14. Esther's prayer for herself and people, 1–19.
15. Esther's approach to the King, 1–16.
16. Letter of Artaxerxes.
    a) 1–9. Pride of exalted persons.
    b) 10–24. The counter decree of the King.]

NEHEMIAH.

PART I. Fortifying and populating Jerusalem, 1–7.

1. Nehemiah's interest in and prayer for the city.
    a) 1–4. His interest in Jerusalem.
    b) 5–11. His prayer for Jerusalem.
2. Removal to Jerusalem.
    a) 1–9. His request for leave of absence.
    b) 10–18. Arrival, measurement and resolve.

3. Names and order of the builders.
   a) 1–5. Enumeration of builders.
   b) 6–32. Enumeration of work.
4. Work with trowel and sword.
   a) 1–6. Ridicule of Tobiah and Sanballat.
   b) 7–14. Precaution against the enemies.
   c) 15–23. Alternate working and watching.
5. Abolition of usury and Nehemiah's unselfishness.
   a) 1–5. People's complaint of oppression.
   b) 6–13. Abolition of usury.
   c) 14–19. Nehemiah's unselfishness.
6. Snares against Nehemiah.
   a) 1–9. Sanballat's attempts against Nehemiah.
   b) 10–14. Sanballat's second attempt against him.
   c) 15–19. Jewish conspiracy against him.
7. Nehemiah's care for the city.
   a) 1–3. Provision for the watching of the city.
   b) 4–38. List of houses and families . . . . Ezra 2: 1–35.
   c) 39–42. List of the priests . . . .   "   36–39.
   d) 43–60. Levites, Nethinim, servants . . . . . .   "   40–60.
   e) 61–65. Unregistered priests . . . . "   61–63.
   f) 66–73. Summary and contributions . . . . "   64–70.

   PART II. Ezra's solemn divine service, 8–10.

8. Reading of the law and keeping of feasts, Ps. 1, 119.
   a) 1–8. Public reading of the law.
   b) 9–12. Feast of the New Moon.
   c) 13–18. Feast of Tabernacles.
9. Day of general fasting and prayer.
   a) 1–8. God's mercy to the patriarchs.
   b) 9–23. Mercy to the wandering nation.
   c) 24–35. Mercy to Israel in Canaan.
   d) 36–38. Renewal of covenant with God.
10. People's covenant and agreement.
    a) 1–32. List of persons who made covenant.
    b) 33–40. Agreement to supply the temple.

    PART III. Various lists and accounts, 11–13.

11. List of inhabitants.
    a) 1–24. Inhabitants of Jerusalem.
    b) 25–36. Inhabitants of towns.
12. Lists and work of officers. Dedication of wall.
    a) 1–21. List of priests.
    b) 22–26. List of heads of Levites.
    c) 27–43. Dedication of the wall.
    d) 44–13:3. Appointment concerning worship.
13. Nehemiah's second visit to Jerusalem.
    a) 4–14. Cleansing and reformation.
    b) 15–22. Sabbath desecration stopped.
    c) 23–31. Marriages with strangers dissolved.

I ESDRAS.   II Chron.

1. Josiah's passover and kings of Judah . . . .   35–36.
   a) 1–21. The great passover of Josiah . . .   . 35: 1–19.
   b) 25–33. Defeat of Josiah by Necho . . . .   35: 20–27.
   c) 34–42. Jechonias (Jehoiakin) . . . . 36: 1–4.
   d) 43–58. Joachim . . . . 36: 5–8.

2. Departure from Babylon.
    a) 1–7. The decree of Cyrus . . . . Ezra, 1 : 1–4.
    b) 8–15. Golden vessels of temple given to Zerubbabel . 1 : 5–11.
    c) 16–24. Letter to Artaxerxes against the Jews . . . . 4 : 7–16.
    d) 25–30. King's answer and consequent hindrance . . 4 : 17–24.
3. The discussion on the strongest thing.
    a) 1–12. The feast and the three opinions.
    b) 13–24. The speech on wine as strongest.
4. Second and third opinions defended and result.
    a) 1–12. Speech on the king.
    b) 13–32. Speech on woman.
    c) 33–40. Speech on truth.
    d) 41–57. Decree to restore Jerusalem.
    e) 58–63. Zerubbabel's thanks.
5. List of returned captives and temple building.
    a) 1–6. Company sent by Darius.
    b) 7–23. List of families . . . . Ezra, 2 : 1–35.
    c) 24–35. Priests, Levites, servants . . . . 2 : 36–60.
    d) 36–46. Unregistered priests and summary . . . . . 2 : 61–72.
    e) 47–55. Restoration of sacrifices . . . . 3 : 1–7.
    f) 56–65. Building encouraged by Levites.
    g) 66–73. The heathens rejected hinder it . . . . 4 : 1–6.
6. The building of temple under Darius.
    a) 1–22. Letter to Darius concerning the temple . . . 5 : 1–17.
    b) 23–26. Decree of Cyrus found . . . . 6 : 1–10.
    c) 27–34. Decree of Darius . . . . 6 : 11–12.
7. The temple completed and passover kept.
    a) 1–9. The completion of the temple . . . . 6 : 13–18.
    b) 10–15. The keeping of the passover . . . . 6 : 19–22.
8. Esdras' (Ezra's) return and commission.
    a) 1–7. Sketch of Ezra . . . . 7 : 1–10.
    b) 8–27. The royal commission . . . . . 7 : 11–28.
    c) 28–40. List of men who returned . . . 8 : 1–14.
    d) 41–53. Priests gotten for the return.
    e) 54–67. Account of the journey . . . . 8 : 15–36.
    f) 68–73. Esdras informed of intermarriages . . . . . 9 : 1–4.
    g) 74–90. Esdras' prayer and confession . . . . 9 : 5–15.
    h) 91–96. Confession in behalf of people . . . . . . 10 : 1–5.
9. Sins removed and law read.
    a) 1–17. The investigation . . . . Ezra, 10 : 6–17.
    b) 18–36. List of the intermarried . . . . " 10 : 18–44.
    c) 37–48. Public reading of the law . . . . Neh., 8 : 1–8.
    d) 49–55. The people comforted . . . . " 8 : 9–12.

II ESDRAS.

PART I. The kingdom taken from the Jews, 1–2.
1. Reproof of the Jews.
    a) 1–3. Genealogies of Esdras (Ezra).
    b) 4–23. Reproof of Israel's thanklessness.
    c) 24–34. Threatened rejection.
    d) 35–40. The kingdom given to the gentiles.
2. Rejection of God. Vision of Son of God.
    a) 1–9. God complains of his people.
    b) 10–33. God's offer to receive them.
    c) 34–41. Exhortation to the Gentiles.
    d) 42–48. Vision of the Son of God.

Part II. Apocalypse, 3–14.

§1. The first vision, 3–5 : 20.
3. Esdras' reflection on Israel's history.
    a) 1–11. Adam to Noah.
    b) 12–22. Abraham to Moses.
    c) 23–36. Troubled at Israel's rejection.
4. Problems of providence.
    a) 1–12. Esdras shown his ignorance by Uriel.
    b) 13–21. Advised not to meddle in things too high.
    c) 22–32. The fruit of wickedness from Adam's evil.
    d) 33–52. Esdras' various questions of Uriel.
5. The future and God's purpose with Israel.
    a) 1–13. The troublous times to come.
    b) 14–20. Esdras' trouble and fasting.

§2. Second vision, 5 : 21–6 : 34.
    c) 21–30. Esdras' question why God punishes chosen people.
    d) 31–49. God's purposes must have time.
    e) 50–56. Succeeding generation of decreasing strength.
6. Israel's rejected condition.
    a) 1–10. God's purpose eternal and unsearchable.
    b) 11–28. The voice predicting the world's end.
    c) 29–34. Esdras advised to fast for another vision.

§3. Third vision, 6 : 35–9 : 25.
    d) 35–59. Israel, for whom all things are made, rejected.
7. The present in relation to the future.
    a) 1–16. The way to great rewards is narrow.
    b) 17–35. The triumph of right.
    c) 36–45. An end of probation coming.
    d) 46–70. Life beyond.
8. Only a chosen few saved.
    a) 1–14. In the case of man in general.
    b) 15–36. Esdras' petition to know about Israel.
    c) 37–44. Analogy of the sown seed.
    d) 45–65. The mystery of the perishing many.
9. The mystery of the righteous' sufferings.
    a) 1–13. There is a time for probation.
    b) 14–25. Few saved out of the many.

§4. Fourth vision, 9 : 26–10 : 58.
    c) 26–37. Israel the perished vessel of God's law.
    d) 38–10 : 4. The vision of the troubled woman.
10. The mourning woman the symbol of Zion.
    a) 5–24. The woman comforted by Esdras.
    b) 25–40. Woman transformed into a city.
    c) 41–59. Explanation of the vision.

§5. Fifth vision. The eagle, 11–12.
11. Conversation of the eagle and the lion.
    a) 1–14. Appearance and reign of the eagle.
    b) 15–35. His reign after his rebuke by a voice.
    c) 36–46. The rebuke from the lion.
12. The vision interpreted.
    a) 1–9. Destruction of the eagle.
    b) 10–39. The interpretation.
    c) 40–51. Israelites seek him and are comforted.

§6. Sixth and seventh visions, 13–14.

13. The sixth vision. The man from the sea.
    a) 1-13.   The vision of the man.
    b) 14-20. Esdras' perplexity over it.
    c) 21-38. Meaning of the warlike multitude.
    d) 39-50. Meaning of peaceful multitude.
    e) 51-58. Mystery of the sea and praise to God.
14. Seventh vision : the voice out of the bush.
    a) 1-18.   The voice from the bush.
    b) 19-26. Desire and charge to write the law.
    c) 27-36. His exhortation to his fellowmen.
    d) 37-48. The law written from his memory.
    PART III. Prophecies against the nations.
15. Prophecy of destruction on Egypt and Asia.
    a) 1-9.   Prophecy of ruin and its cause.
    b) 10-27. Egypt to be troubled.
    c) 28-45. The vision of horror.
    d) 46-63. Woes pronounced on Asia.
16. Great desolation coming.
    a) 1-16.   Irresistable woes coming.
    b) 17-34. Description of the coming woe.
    c) 35-52. Conduct in view of the danger.
    d) 53-78. Confession and repentance advised.

MALACHI : REBUKES AGAINST PRIESTS AND PEOPLE.

1. Priests' offerings rejected.
    a) 1-5.   Israel is shown God's love.
    b) 6-14.   Rebuke and rejection.
2. Rebukes for partiality and unlawful marriages.
    a) 1-9.   Rebuke for partiality.
    b) 9-17.   Rebukes for unlawful marriages.
3 and 4. The coming of the God of judgment.
    a) 1-5.   Coming in judgment.
    b) 6-12.   Unbelief shuts out God.
    c) 13-4 : 6. Distinction between the good and bad.

EPOCH II. INTERTESTAMENTARY HISTORY, 400-4.

21. THE GRECIAN PERIOD, 333-168.

Hurlbut, pages 94-96.

ECCLESIASTICUS.

Preface : Origin of the book.
Prologue : Book written for instruction in the law.
1. The beginning of wisdom.
    a) 1-10.   The origin of wisdom is in God.
    b) 11-19. The blessings of wisdom.
    c) 20-30. Its entrance into man's heart.
2. The wise man is patient in trouble.
    a) 1-5.   Trouble must come.
    b) 6-18.   How to receive trouble.
3. The wisdom of filial affection and humility.
    a) 1-16.   Wisdom of honoring father and mother.
    b) 17-31. Wisdom of humility.
4. Charity, getting wisdom, ashamed.
    a) 1-10.   Wisdom as charity.
    b) 11-19. Wisdom's ways with her pupils.
    c) 20-31. What to be ashamed of.

5. The folly of presumption, 1-15.
6. Friendship and getting wisdom.
    a) 1-17. On friendship.
    b) 18-37. Exhortation to get wisdom.
7. Miscellaneous exhortations.
8. Miscellaneous proverbs.
9. Women and associates.
    a) 1-9. Warnings against women.
    b) 10-18. Concerning associates.
10. Humility and the fear of God, 1-31.
11. Proverbs on wealth, etc.
12. One's relation to the wicked.
    a) 1-9. Not to give alms to the ungodly.
    b) 10-18. Be wary of enemies.
13. The high and the low.
    a) 1-14. Associate not with proud superiors.
    b) 15-26. The rich despise the poor.
14. On liberality and wisdom.
    a) 1-16. Advice on liberality.
    b) 17-27. Advice to search wisdom.
15. Concerning wisdom and folly (sin).
    a) 1-10. Blessings of wisdom.
    b) 11-20. Sin and folly are our own choice.
16. The sure punishment of the wicked.
    a) 1-17. God unmerciful to the ungodly.
    b) 17-30. His doings are marvelous.
17. God and man.
    a) 1-13. Man's creation and endowment.
    b) 14-30. Man's deeds seen of God.
18. Proverbs and precepts.
    a) 1-14. What man is and his relation to God.
    b) 15-33. Precepts for man's doings.
19. Pleasure and talking about persons.
    a) 1-5. Sins of pleasure.
    b) 6-17. Talking about neighbors.
    c) 18-30. Sin and folly.
20. Proverbs, mostly on speaking.
21. Sins, folly and wisdom, 1-32.
    a) 1-11. Proverbs on sins.
    b) 12-28. The fool and the wise man.
22. Proverbs, mostly on folly, 1-27.
23. Proverbs, mostly on swearing and adultery.
    a) 1-15. Mostly on swearing.
    b) 16-28. On adultery.
24. Wisdom's discourse on herself (cf. Prov. 8).
25. Mostly on wisdom and woman.
    a) 1-12. On wisdom.
    b) 13-26. On woman (especially the wicked).
26. On good and bad women.
27. Proverbs on human conduct, 1-30.
28. Mostly concerning slander and strife, 1-26.
29. On surety and neighborliness, 1-28.
30. Proverbs on children and health.
    a) 1-13. Bringing up of children.
    b) 14-25. Blessing of health and cheerfulness.
31. Riches and moderation.
    a) 1-11. On riches.
    b) 12-31. Moderation in eating and drinking.

32. Conduct in company and toward self.
    a) 1–13. Social etiquette.
    b) 14–24. Conduct toward ourself.
33. God's dealings with men and men with each other.
    a) 1–16. God's dealings with men, &c.
    b) 17–31. Relation to our children and servants.
34. On dreams, wisdom and worship.
    a) 1–8. On dreams.
    b) 9–17. Wisdom by traveling.
    c) 18–26. What worship is acceptable.
35. Behavior toward God and man.
    a) 1–11. What to sacrifice.
    b) 12–20. Judge for the widows.
36. Prayer for Israel. Woman.
    a) 1–17. Prayer for Israel's restoration
    b) 18–26. Concerning women.
37. On counsellors and wisdom.
    a) 1–15. Whom to consult.
    b) 16–31. Advice.
38. Physicians, mourning, craftsmen.
    a) 1–15. Concerning physicians.
    b) 16–23. How to mourn.
    c) 24–34. Usefulness of the callings of life.
39. Result of a study of God's words and works.
    a) 1–11. The student of the bible.
    b) 12–21. Exhortation to praise God.
    c) 22–35. All God's works for a purpose.
40. Wicked men's punishments and comparisons.
    a) 1–17. Life has miseries especially for sinners.
    b) 18–30. Things " better than both," &c.
41. Of the ungodly and what to be ashamed of.
    a) 1–13. Of the ungodly.
    b) 14–24. Of what to be ashamed.
42. Things to be ashamed of and works of God.
    a) 1–8. What to be ashamed of.
    b) 9–14. Parental care for daughter.
    c) 15–25. The works of God.
43. Praise of God's glorious works.
    a) 1–12. The heavenly host.
    b) 13–26. Winds and weather.
    c) 27–33. God is great in his works.

Praise of Famous Men, 40–50.

44. Of men down to Jacob.
    a) 1–15. Of great men in general.
    b) 16–23. Enoch, Abraham and Jacob.
45. Moses, Aaron and Phinehas.
    a) 1–5. Praise of Moses.
    b) 6–22. Praise of Aaron.
    c) 23–26. Praise of Phinehas.
46. History from Joshua to Samuel.
    a) 1–8. Of Joshua.
    b) 9–20. Caleb, Judges and Samuel.
47. David, Solomon, Rehoboam and Jeroboam.
    a) 1–11. Life and works of David.
    b) 12–22. Life and works of Solomon.
    c) 23–25. Rehoboam and Jeroboam.

48. Elijah, Elisha and Hezekiah.
    a) 1-11. Life and works of Elijah.
    b) 12-16. Life and works of Elisha.
    c) 17-24. Life and works of Hezekiah.
49. Josiah and others.
    a) 1-10. Josiah and Ezekiel.
    b) 11-16. Various other men.
50. Praise of the High Priest Simon.
    a) 1-12. His personal appearance.
    b) 13-21. His official work.
    c) 22-28. Prayer for God's blessing.
51. Prayer of Jesus, son of Sirach.
    a) 1-12. Thanksgiving for deliverance.
    b) 13-22. His search for wisdom.
    c) 23-30. Instruction offered to learners.

22. PERIOD OF JEWISH INDEPENDENCE, 168-63.

Antiochus Epiphanes to Pompey.

Hurlbut, pages 96-100.

I MACCABEES.

PART I. History of Mattathias, 1-2. B. C. 167-161.

1. The abominations of Antiochus.
    a) 1-10. Division of Alexander's kingdom.
    b) 11-15. Heathenizing tendencies of Jews.
    c) 16-28. Jerusalem desecrated by Antiochus.
    d) 29-40. Jerusalem captured by Antiochus.
    e) 41-51. The decree of Antiochus to unify all customs.
    f) 52-64. Persecution of the Jews.
2. The work of Mattathias.
    a) 1-14. Mattathias' lament over Jerusalem.
    b) 15-26. His zeal for the law.
    c) 27-38. He is attacked on the Sabbath.
    d) 39-48. Resolution to fight on Sabbath and success.
    e) 49-70. Mattathias' dying charge to his sons.

PART II. History of Judas, 3-9: 22. B. C. 161-143.

3. The beginning of Judas' success . . . . II Macc. 8: 1-35.
    a) 1-9. Character of Judas and his work . .   8: 1-7.
    b) 10-26. The battle against Apollonius and at Bethhoron.
    c) 27-37. Antiochus' expedition across Euphrates.
    d) 38-60. Prayer and fasting before the battle of Emmaus.
4. Defeat of the enemy and temple cleansing.
    a) 1-25. Gorgias defeated by the Jews at Emmaus.
    b) 26-35. Lysias defeated at Bethsura . . II Macc. 11: 1-38.
    c) 36-51. The cleansing of the temple .
    d) 52-61. Dedication of the new altar . .   10: 1-9.
5. Battles in Galilee and Gilead . . .   . . II Macc. 10-38 and 12.
    a) 1-8. Heathens defeated in the south.
    b) 9-20. Call for help from Gilead and Galilee.
    c) 21-36. Gilead delivered from Timotheus.
    d) 37-44. Timotheus defeated a second time.
    e) 45-54. Removal of Gileadites to Judea.
    f) 55-68. Juda's superiority over his brethren.

6. Death of Antiochus and connected events.
    a) 1-17. Antiochus' grief and death. II Macc. 9: 1-29.
    b) 18-27. Renegade Jews petition the king.
    c) 28-47. Jews defeated by (Lysias under) Eupater.
    d) 48-54. Events about Jerusalem and Bethsura.
    e) 55-63. Treaty made and broken by Lysias.
7. Fights with Demetrius, Alcimus and Nicanor. I Macc. 14.
    a) 1-20. Demetrius attacks the Jews.
    b) 21-25. Alcimus' attack on the Jews.
    c) 26-38. Nicanor's treachery and insolence.
    d) 39-50. Nicanor defeated after prayer.
8. Intercourse with the Romans.
    a) 1-16. Description of the Romans.
    b) 17-32. The treaty with the Romans.
9. Death of Judas and election of Jonathan.
    a) 1-22. Defeat and death of Judas.

PART III. History of Jonathan, 9: 23-12. B. C. 161-143.

    b) 23-31. Election of Jonathan as leader.
10. Jonathan's rejection of Demetrius and alliance with Alexander.
    a) 1-14. Demetrius makes a treaty with Jonathan.
    b) 15-21. Jonathan called king's friend by Alexander.
    c) 22-45. Overtures of alliance from Demetrius.
    d) 46-66. Marriage of Cleopatra and honor of Jonathan.
    e) 67-73. Challenge from Demetrius II.
    f) 74-89. Demetrius II defeated by Jonathan.
11. Time of Alexander, Demetrius and Antiochus, Jr.
    a) 1-12. Ptolemy's attempt to take Syria from Alexander.
    b) 13-19. Death of Alexander and Ptolemy. Ascent of Demetrius.
    c) 20-37. Jonathan favored by Demetrius II.
    d) 38-53. Demetrius II saved by Jonathan.
    e) 54-74. Jonathan's exploits for Antiochus, Jr.
12. Jonathan's exploits and death.
    a) 1-5.   Renewal of treaty with Rome.
    b) 6-23. Renewal of treaty with Sparta.
    c) 24-38. Jonathan wards off the foes and builds Jerusalem.
    d) 39-53. Jonathan deceived and captured.

PART IV. The history of Simon, 13-16. B. C. 143-135.

13. Simon's first works.
    a) 1-11. Simon assumes the leadership.
    b) 12-24. Tryphon's futile attempt to invade Juda.
    c) 25-35. Monuments and strongholds built by Simon.
    d) 36-42. Peace established between Jews and Demetrius.
    e) 43-53. Gaza besieged and Jerusalem delivered.
14. Simon's prosperous reign.
    a) 1-14. Peace and prosperity of Juda.
    b) 15-24. Treaty between Romans and Simon.
    c) 25-49. Brass memorial tablets in honor of Simon.
15. Negotiations of Antiochus VI with Jews.
    a) 1-14. Antiochus Sidetes favors the Jews and defeats Tryphon.
    b) 15-24. Circular letter from Rome in favor of the Jews.
    c) 25-41. Antiochus' quarrel with Simon.
16. Wars with Cendebaeus and Ptolemy.
    a) 1-10. Defeat of Cendebaeus by Judas and John.
    b) 11-22. Ptolemy's attempt to gain Judea.

II MACCABEES.

PART I. Two letters to Egypt.
1. Celebration of the feast of tabernacles.
    a) 1–9. Letter urging Egyptian Jews to keep feast.
    b) 10–18. Death of Antiochus.
    c) 19–36. Preservation of the sacred fire.
2. The feast of dedication and plan of this book.
    a) 1–8. The hiding of the ark by Jeremiah.
    b) 9–18. Exhortation to keep feast of dedication.
    c) 19–32. The author's plan and purpose.

PART II. Troubles from within and without, 3–10:9.
3. The fortunes of the temple through Heliodorus.
    a) 1–6. Temple treasures betrayed by Simon.
    b) 7–13. Heliodorus sent to plunder the temple.
    c) 14–30. Heliodorus chastised by God.
    d) 31–40. His miraculous healing.
4. Evil doings of Jason and Menelaus.
    a) 1–6. Onias slandered by Simon.
    b) 7–17. Jason hellenizing the Jews.
    c) 18–22. Jason's favors to the rulers.
    d) 23–38. Menelaus buys the priesthood and kills Onias.
    e) 39–50. Popular uprising against Menelaus.
5. False report of death of Antiochus.
    a) 1–10. The end of Jason.
    b) 11–20. The devastations of Antiochus.
    c) 21–27. Subjugation of Jerusalem.
6. Jews' fidelity to the law.
    a) 1–11. Antiochus' attempt to heathenize the Jews.
    b) 12–17. The author's reflection on these events.
    c) 18–31. Martyrdom of Eleazar.
7. Martyrdom of a mother with her seven sons.
    a) 1–19. Horrible torture and death of six sons.
    b) 20–29. The youngest encouraged by his mother.
    c) 30–42. Rebuking the King, he dies with his mother.
8. Judas' victory over Nicanor.
    a) 1–7. The beginning of Judas' work.
    b) 8–15. Nicanor's march against Judas.
    c) 16–20. Judas exhorts his men.
    d) 21–29. Judas defeats Nicanor.
    e) 30–36. Success of Judas' generals.
9. Death of Antiochus.
    a) 1–18. Divine visitation on him.
    b) 19–27. His letter to the Jews.
    c) 28–29. His death.
10. Judas' work at temple and against foes.
    a) 1–9. Cleansing of the temple.

PART III. Jewish victories, 10:10–15.

    b) 10–13. Reign of Eupater.
    c) 14–23. Campaign against the Idumeans.
    d) 24–38. Victory over Timotheus.
11. Defeat of Lysias and treaty with Syria and Rome.
    a) 1–16. Defeat of the army under Lysias.
    b) 17–38. Correspondence and treaty with Syrians and Romans.

12. Syrian faithlessness to the treaty.
    a) 1-9. Judas punishes Joppa and Jamnia.
    b) 10-16. Victories of Arabians and the city Caspis.
    c) 17-25. Defeat of the army under Timotheus.
    d) 26-31. Carnion won and Feast of Weeks kept.
    e) 32-45. Victory, or Idumeans retarded by idolatry.
13. Antiochus Eupater defeated by Judas.
    a) 1-8. Death of Menelaus in ashes.
    b) 9-17. The King's army surprised and slain.
    c) 18-26. His treaty with the Jews renewed.
14. Nicanor's generalship over Judea. (I Macc. 7.)
    a) 1-14. War stirred up by Alcimus.
    b) 15-36. Nicanor's treaty. Alcimus' treachery.
    c) 37-46. Accusation and self destruction of Razis.
15. The crowning success of Judas.
    a) 1-16. Judas encourages his men.
    b) 17-24. The meeting of the armies.
    c) 25-36. Nicanor defeated and slain.
    d) 37-39. The author's conclusion.

BARUCH.

1. Introduction and confession.
    a) 1-14. Introduction.
    b) 15-22. Confession.
2. Israel's prayer to God.
    a) 1-9. God's punishment acknowledged.
    b) 10-35. Prayer for deliverance.
3. On wisdom.
    a) 1-8. Invocation.
    b) 9-23. Wisdom not found on earth.
    c) 24-39. Not to the strong but to Israel did God give it.
4. Personified Jerusalem's address to her sons.
    a) 1-20. Jerusalem charges its people with sin.
    b) 21-29. She encourages her people to hope.
    c) 30-37. She is encouraged to hope.
5. The coming glory of Jerusalem, 1-9
6. Letter of Jeremiah: folly and sin of idol worship, 1-73.

WISDOM OF SOLOMON. (Smith's Bib. Dict.)

PART I. Wisdom moral and intellectual, 1-9.

§1. Wisdom the source of immortality, 1-5.
1. Condition of wisdom. Source of sin.
    a) 1-11. The conditions of wisdom.
    b) 12-16. Actual sin by man's free will.
2. The blindness of the sensualist.
    a) 1-20. The reasoning of the sensualist.
    b) 21-24. Source of sin is in the devil.
3 and 4. The godly and wicked in life.
    a) 1-10. In chastisements.
    b) 11-4:6. In their offspring.
    c) 7-20. In length of life.
5. The godly and the wicked after death.
    a) 1-14. The judgment of conscience.
    b) 15-23. The judgment of God.
        §2. Wisdom the guide of life, 6-9.

6. Wisdom the guide of princes.
    a) 1–11. The responsibility of power.
    b) 12–16. Wisdom soon found.
    c) 17–21. Source of true sovereignty.
7. Realm of wisdom.
    a) 6 : 22–7 : 7. Open to all.
    b) 8–8 : 1. Pervading all creation.
8. Wisdom swaying all life and is gift of God.
    a) 2–17. Swaying all life.
    b) 18–21. Only from God.
9. Prayer for wisdom.
    a) 1–12. Petition for wisdom and its use.
    b) 13 -18. Needed to please God.
   PART II. Wisdom in history, 10 -19.
        § 1. Wisdom a power to save and chastise, 10–12.
10. Wisdom seen in the guidance of Israel.
    a) 1–9. Adam to Abraham.
    b) 10–11 : 4. Jacob and his descendants.
11. In punishment of Egyptians.
    a) 5–14. Egypt punished wherein Israel blessed.
    b) 15–26. God does not lack means to punish.
12. Punishment of Canaanites and lessons of mercy.
    a) 2–18. Punishment of Canaanites.
    b) 19–27. Lesson of mercy and judgment.
        § 2. Growth of idolatry vs. wisdom, 13–14.
13. Worship of nature and images.
    a) 1-9. Worship of nature.
    b) 10-19. Wretchedness of image worship.
14. Worship of images and men, with its effect.
    a) 1–13. Folly of image worship.
    b) 14–21. Worship of deified men.
    c) 22–31. Moral effect of idolatry.
        § 3. True worship vs. idolaters, 15–19.
15. General contrast, 1–17.
16. At the Exodus in beasts and water, etc.
    a) 15 : 18–16 : 13. The actions of beasts.
    b) 14–29. Actions of water and fire.
17. At the Exodus: Symbolic darkness.
    a) 1–10. Reason and nature of the punishment.
    b) 11–21. Terrors of an evil conscience.
18. At the Exodus: the action of death.
    a) 1–17. Why Egypt was punished.
    b) 18–26. Plague of Israel stayed.
19. Contrast between Israel and Egypt.
    a) 1–17. Reason for treatment of Egypt.
    b) 18–22. Conclusion.

EPOCH III. NEW TESTAMENT HISTORY.
23. LIFE OF CHRIST.

Hurlbut, pages 100–111.	Matt.	Mark.	Luke.	John.
§1. THE PREPARATION. 30 YEARS	1–2		1–2	1:1–18
1) Prefaces			1:1–4	
2) Announcement of birth of John Baptist			1:5–25	
3) Announcement of birth of Jesus			1:26–38	
4) Mary's visit to Elizabeth			1:39–56	
5) Birth of John Baptist			1:57–80	
6) Annunciation to Joseph	1:18–25			
7) Birth of Jesus			2:1–7	
8) The genealogies	1:1–17		3:23–38	
9) Annunciation to the shepherds			2:8–20	
10) Presentation in the temple			2:21–39	
11) Visit of the Magi	2:1–12			
12) Flight into Egypt	2:13–15			
13) Slaughter of the children	2:16–18			
14) Sojourn at Nazareth	2:19–23		2:39–40	
15) Jesus' visit to the temple			2:41–52	
§2. THE INAUGURATION. 15 MONTHS.	3–4:12	1:1–14	3–4:15	1:19–c4
1) Ministry of John Baptist	3:1–12	1:1–8	3:1–18	
2) Baptism of Jesus	3:13–17	1:9–11	3:21–23	1:32
3) The temptation	4:1–11	1:12–13	4:1–13	
4) The testimony of John Baptist				1:19–34
5) First disciples of Jesus				1:35–51
6) The wedding at Cana				2:1–12
7) Jesus' first cleansing of the temple				2:13–25
8) Jesus and Nicodemus				3:1–21
9) Renewed testimony of John				3:22–36
10) Journey through Samaria	4:12	1:14	4:14	4:1–42
§3. EARLY GALILEAN MINISTRY. 4 MO.	4:13–7	1:15-3:19	4:16–6	5
1) Cordial reception in Galilee	4:17	1:15–15	4:14–15	4:43–45
2) Healing of nobleman's son				4:46–54
3) Rejection at Nazareth			4:16–30	
4) Settlement at Capernaum	4:13–16		4:31–32	
5) Public calling of four disciples	4:18–22	1:16–20	5:1–11	
6) Sabbath at Capernaum	8:14–17	1:21–34	4:31–41	
7) First circuit through Galilee	4:23	1:35–39	4:42–44	
8) Cleansing of the leper	8:2–4	1:40–45	5:12–16	
9) Healing of the paralytic	9:2–8	2:1–12	5:17–26	
10) Call of Matthew and his feast	9:9–17	2:13–22	5:27–39	
11) Healing of the impotent man				5:1–47
12) The Sabbath question	12:1–14	2:23-3:6	6:1–11	
13) Many followers	12:15–21	3:7–12		
14) The twelve appointed	10:2–4	3:13–19	6:12–19	
15) The sermon on the mount	5:1–8:1		6:20–49	
§4. THE LATER GALILEAN MINISTRY, 10 MONTHS	8–14	3:19–6	7–9:17	6
1) Centurion's servant healed	8:5–13		7:1–11	
2) Widow's son raised			7:11–17	
3) Message from John Baptist	11:2–19		7:18–35	
4) Jesus the guest of Simon			7:36–50	
5) Second circuit through Galilee			8:1–3	
6) Blind and dumb demoniac healed	12:22-37	3:19–30	11:14–23	

	Matt.	Mark.	Luke.	John.
7) Pharisees demand a sign	12:38-45		11:16,24-36	
8) His disciples are his true kinsmen	12:46-50	3:31-35	8:19-21	
9) Parable of the sower	13:1-23	4:1-25	8:4-18	
10) Parables of the kingdom of heaven	13:24-53	4:26-34		
11) The stilling of the tempest	8:18 27	4:35-41	8:22-25	
12) The Gadarene demoniacs	8:28-9:1	5:1-21	8:26-40	
13) Raising of Jairus' daughter	9:18-26	5:21-43	8:40-56	
14) Two blind men and a dumb spirit	9:27-34			
15) Second rejection at Nazareth	13:54-58	6:1-6		
16) Third circuit through Galilee The twelve sent forth	} 9:35-11:1	6:6-13	9:1-6	
17) Herod's opinion of Jesus	14:1-12	6:14-29	9:7-9	
18) The twelve return, 5000 fed	14:13-21	6:30-44	9:10-17	6:1-14
19) Jesus walks upon the water	14:22-36	6:45-56		6:15-21
20) Discourse on the bread of life				16:22-71
§5. THE RETIREMENT, SIX MONTHS	15-18	7-9	9:18-50	
1) Ceremonial traditions	15:1-20	7:1-23		
2) Syrophœnician woman's daughter cured	15:21-28	7:24-30		
3) Deaf and dumb man cured	15:29-31	7:31-37		
4) Feeding the four thousand	15:32-39	8:1-9		
5) Sign again demanded	15:39-16:4	8:10-12		
6) The leaven of the Pharisees	16:4-12	8:13-21		
7) Healing of the blind man		8:22-26		
8) Peter's confession	16:13-20	8:27-30	9:18-21	
9) Prediction of death and resurrection	16:21-28	8:31-9:1	9:22-27	
10) The transfiguration	17:1-13	9:2-13	9:28-36	
11) The demoniac boy healed	17:14-21	9:14-29	9:37-43	
12) Second prediction of death	17:22-23	9:30-32	9:43-45	
13) The tribute money	17:24-27	9:33		
14) The disciples' ambition rebuked, etc.,	18:1-9	9:33-50	9:46-50	
15) Parables on forgiveness	18:10-35			
§6. THE JUDEAN MINISTRY, FOUR MO.			9:51-13:21	7-10
1) Final departure from Galilee	19:1	10:1	9:51-56	7:1-10
2) Test of discipleship		8:19-22	9:57-62	
3) The seventy sent forth			10:1-12	
4) Ten lepers healed			17:11-19	
5) Jesus' discourses at Jerusalem				7:11-53
6) The adulteress forgiven				8:1-11
7) Further discourses at Jerusalem				8:12-59
8) The blind man healed on Sabbath				9:1-10:21
9) Return of the seventy	11:25-30		10:17-24	
10) Parable of the good Samaritan			10:25-37	
11) Jesus the guest of Martha and Mary			10:38-42	
12) The disciples again taught to pray			11:1-13	
13) Woes on Pharisees and lawyers			11:37-54	
14) Against hypocrisy and timidity			12:1-12	
15) Against covetousness			12:13-34	
16) Parable of the unfaithful servant			12:35-59	
17) Lesson from slaying of Galileans			13:1-9	
18) Healing the infirm woman			13 10-21	
19) Jesus at feast of Dedication				10:22-42
§7. THE PEREAN MINISTRY. 4 MO.	19-20	10	13 21-19:28	11-12:11
1) Journey toward Jerusalem	19:1-2	10:1	13 22-35	
2) Jesus, guest of chief Pharisee			14:1-24	
3) What is required of true disciples			14:25-35	

		Matt.	Mark.	Luke.	John.
4)	Lost sheep, money and son			15 : 1–32	
5)	Parable of the unjust steward			16 : 1–13	
6)	Parable of rich man and Lazarus . .			16 14-31	
7)	Forbearance, faith and humility			17 : 1–10	
8)	The raising of Lazarus				11 : 1–46
9)	Jews counsel Jesus' death				11 : 47-57
10)	The coming of the kingdom			17 : 20-37	
11)	Importunate widow. Penitent publican			18 : 1–14	
12)	Concerning divorce	19 : 3–12	10 : 2–12		
13)	Jesus receives little children	19 : 13-15	10 : 13-16	18 : 15-17	
14)	Rich young man	19 : 16-30	10 : 17-31	18 : 18-30	
15)	Parable of the laborers	20 : 1–16			
16)	Jesus' third prediction of his death . .	22 : 17-19	10 : 33-34	18 : 31-34	
17)	Ambition of James and John	20 : 20-28	10 : 35-45		
18)	Healing of two blind men	20 : 29-34	10 : 46-52	18 : 35-43	
19)	Visit to Zaccheus			19 : 1–10	
20)	Parable of the ten pounds			19 : 11-28	
21)	Arrival at Bethany	26 : 6–13	14 : 3–9		11:55-12:11
§8.	THE PASSION WEEK	21–27	11–15	19 : 29-23	12–19
	a) *Sunday, April 2, A. D. 30.*				
1)	Triumphant entry into Jerusalem . .	21 : 1–11	11 : 1–10	19 : 29-44	12 : 12-19
	b) *Monday, April 3.*				
2)	The fig tree cursed	21 : 18-19	11 : 12-14		
3)	The temple cleansed	21 : 12-17	11 : 15-19	19 : 45-48	
	c) *Tuesday, April 4.*				
4)	Fig tree found withered	21 : 20-22	11 : 20-26		
5)	Christ's authority questioned	21 : 23-32	11 : 27-33	20 : 1–8	
6)	Parable of the wicked husbandmen .	21 : 33-46	12 : 1–12	20 : 9–19	
7)	Parable of the wedding garment . .	22 : 1–14			
8)	Catch questions to Jesus	22 : 15-46	12 : 13-37	20 : 20-44	
9)	Denunciation of the Pharisees . . .	23 : 13-39	12 : 40	20 : 47	
10)	The widow's mite		12 : 41–44	21 : 1–4	
11)	Jesus' interview with certain Greeks .				12 : 20–36
12)	Unbelief of the Jews				12 : 37–50
13)	Destruction of Jerusalem foretold . .	24 : 1-31	13 : 1–27	21 : 5–28	
14)	Watchfulness enforced	24 : 32-51	13 : 28-37	21 : 29–36	
15)	Parable of the virgins and talents . .	25 : 1–30			
16)	Final judgment foretold	25 : 31-46			
17)	Betrayal announced	26 : 1–2	14 : 1	22 : 1	
	d) *Wednesday, April 5.*				
18)	Conspiracy against Christ	26 : 3–16	14 : 1–11	22 : 2–6	
	(Jesus in retirement at Bethany.)				
	e) *Thursday, April 6.*				
19)	Preparation for the passover	26 : 17-19	14 : 12–16	22 : 7–13	
20)	Contention at the passover meal . .	26 : 20	14 : 17	22 : 14–30	
21)	Jesus washes the disciples' feet . . .				13 : 1–20
22)	Jesus points out the traitor	26 : 21-25	14 : 18–21	22 : 21–23	13 : 21–35
23)	Lord's supper instituted	26 : 26-29	14 : 22–25	22 : 19–20	11 : 23–36
24)	Peter's denial foretold	26 : 30-35	14 : 26–31	22 : 31–38	13 : 36–38
25)	Jesus comforts his disciples . . .				14 : 1–31
26)	Christ the true vine				15 : 1–27
27)	Persecution, promise of the spirit . .				16 : 1–33
28)	Christ's high priestly prayer				17 : 1–26
29)	Jesus goes to Gethsemane	26 : 30	14 : 26	22 : 39	18 : 1
30)	The agony in Gethsemane	26 : 36-46	14 : 32–42	22 : 40–46	18 : 1

83

| | Matt. | Mark. | Luke. | John. |

f) *Friday, April 7.*
31) Jesus betrayed and arrested 26: 47-56 14: 43–52 22: 47–48 18: 2–12
32) Jesus before Annas, the Caiaphas . . 26: 57-75 14: 53–72 22: 54–71
33) Before Sanhedrin at daybreak . . . 27: 1-2 15: 1 22: 66–71
34) Judas repents and hangs himself . . 27: 3-10
35) Jesus before Pilate 27: 11–14 15: 1–5 23: 1–5 18: 28–38
36) Before Herod and return to Pilate . 23: 6–16
37) Jesus scourged, Barabbas released . . 27: 15-26 15.: 6–15 23: 17–25 18: 39–40
38) Jesus mocked by soldiers 27: 27-30 15: 16–19 19: 1–3
39) Pilate's last effort to release Jesus . . 19: 4–16
40) Jesus led away to be crucified . . . 27: 31-34 15: 20–23 23: 26–33 19: 16–17
41) The crucifixion 27: 35-38 15: 24–28 23: 33,34-38 19: 18–24
42) Jews mock Jesus 27: 39-44 15: 29–32 23: 35–43
43) Jesus commends his mother to John, 19: 25–27
44) Darkness and death of Jesus . . 27: 45-50 15: 33–37 23: 44–46 19: 28–30
45) Signs and wonders, etc. 27: 51-56 15: 38-41 23: 45-49 19: 31-37
46) The burial 27: 57-61 15: 42-47 23: 50-56 19: 38-42
g) *Saturday, Jewish Sabbath, April 8*
47) The sepulchre sealed and guarded . . 27: 62-66

§9. THE RESURRECTION. 40 DAYS.
i) *Sunday, April 9.*
1) Jesus appeared to Mary Magdalene . 16: 1–9 20: 1–18
2) To some women with "All Hail" . 28: 1–15 16: 10-11
3) On the way to Emaus 16: 12-13 24: 1–33
4) To Simon Peter 24: 34
5) To the ten—Thomas absent . . . 16: 4 24: 36-43 20: 19-25
j) *Later appearances.*
6) To the eleven—Thomas present . . 20: 26-31
7) To seven disciples near sea of Galilee 21: 1–25
8) To 500 in Galilee . . . . 28: 16-20 16: 15-18 (I Cor. 15:6)
9) To James, the Lord's brother . . . . (" 15:7)
10) Near Bethany. The ascension . . . 16: 19-20 24: 44-53 (Acts 1:4-12)

24. PETRINE PERIOD. JEWISH CHRISTIANITY, Acts 1–12.

A. D. 33.   Hurlbut, pages 112–115.

§1. THE FOUNDING OF THE CHURCH, Acts 1–2.
1. Antecedents of the founding.
   a) 1–14. The Ascension of Jesus.
   b) 15–26. Choice of an apostle.
2. The founding of the church.
   a) 1–13. The outpouring of the spirit.
   b) 14–36. Peter's sermon.
   c) 37–41. The effect of the sermon.
   d) 42–47. State of the primitive church described.

§2. THE CHURCH IN JERUSALEM, Acts 3–7.
3. Healing the lame man, and Peter's address.
   a) 1–10. Healing of the lame man.
   b) 11–26. Peter's temple address.
4. Arrest and release of Peter and John.
   b) 1–4. Arrest of Peter and John.
   b) 5–22. Peter and John before the Sanhedrin.
   c) 23–31. The prayer of the disciples.
   d) 32–37. Second description of the church.

5. Divine protection of the church.
      a) 1–11. Wickedness in the church punished.
      b) 12–16. Public opinion of the church.
      c) 17–32. Peter's arrest and deliverance.
      d) 33–42. Intervention of Gamaliel.
   6. Deacons chosen. Stephen.
      a) 1–7. The choice of seven men.
      b) 8–15. The work and accusation of Stephen.
   7. Stephen's address and death.
      a) 1–16. Age of the Patriarchs.
      b) 17–43. Age of Moses.
      c) 44–53. Post-Mosaic time.
      d) 54–8 : 1. Stoning of Stephen.

§3. THE CHURCH IN JUDEA, SAMARIA AND ANTIOCH, Acts 8–12.

   8. Growth through persecution.
      a) 1–8. Persecution spreads the church.
      b) 9–25. Simon Magus.
      c) 26–40. Conversion of the Ethiopian eunuch.
   9. Conversion of Paul and work of Peter.
      a) 1–19. The conversion of Saul.
      b) 19–30. The first preaching of Saul.
      c) 31–43. Work of Peter in Lydda and Joppa.
  10. The church opened to the Gentiles.
      a) 1–8. Cornelius' vision.
      b) 9–16. Peter's vision.
      c) 17–33. Cornelius sends for and receives Peter.
      d) 34–43. Peter's address.
      e) 44–48. The Spirit given to heathen.
  11. The entrance of Gentiles confirmed.
      a) 1–18. Peter's vindication in Jerusalem.
      b) 19–26. Founding of a Gentile congregation in Antioch.
      c) 27–30. Agabus predicts a famine.
  12. Persecution under Herod.
      a) 1–5. Execution of James and arrest of Peter.
      b) 6–17. Miraculous deliverance of Peter.
      c) 18–25. Fate of Herod. Saul's return to Antioch.

§4. EPISTLES: TO JEWISH CHRISTIANS.

Jude. Defense of the faith.
   a) 1–4. Introduction.
   b) 5–19. False teachers judged already.
   c) 20–25. Exhortation and doxology.

James. Exhortation to Christian practice.
   1. Endurance of trials.
      a) 2–12. Steadfastness in trials.
      b) 13–18. The source of temptation.
      c) 19–27. Exhortation to do the word.
   2. Faith working by love.
      a) 1–13. Love to poor as well as rich.
      14–26. Faith without works is dead.
   3. Control of the tongue a mark of wisdom.
   4. Strife and evil speaking.
   5. Sins of the rich and conclusion.
      a) 1–11. Rich rebuked and poor comforted.
      b) 12–20. Various exhortations.

I PETER. "Stand Fast in the Faith."

Part I. The Christian's blessings, 1–2: 10.
1. Hope, holiness and love.
   a) 1–12. The inheritance beyond present trial.
   b) 13–21. "Holy in all manner of living."
   c) 22–25. Fervent brotherly love.
2. Lively stones. Submission.
   a) 1–10. Living stones in spiritual temple.
   Part II. The Christian's duties, 2: 11–5.
   b) 11–17. Blameless life and submission to superiors.
   c) 18–25. Submission to masters good or bad.
3. Behavior in good and evil fellowship.
   a) 1–8. Relation between man and wife.
   b) 9-22. Endurance of cruelty and wrong.
4. Steadfastness, temperance and patience.
   a) 1–6. Not return to Gentile lusts.
   b) 7–11. Temperance and love.
   c) 12–19. Blessedness of unjustly suffering.
5. Concluding words.
   a) 1–4. Exhortation to the elders.
   b) 5–9. Exhortation to the members.
   c) 10–14. Doxology and salutations.

II PETER. Knowledge not Fables as Scoffers Say.
1. The foundations of Christian hope.
   a) 1–11. Attainment of full Christian knowledge.
   b) 12–21. Certainty of Christ's second coming.
2. The libertines and their punishment, 1–22.
3. God's long-suffering.
   a) 1–7. Warnings against scoffers.
   b) 8–13. Reason for delay of judgment.
   c) 14–18. Difficulties of Paul's letter. Conclusion.

HEBREWS. New Dispensation Superior to the Old.
Part I. Christ's superiority over all mediators, 1–4.
1. His superiority over angels.
   a) 1–4. The thesis.
   b) 5–14. His superiority over angels.
2. Exaltation of humanity.
   a) 1–5. Be firm in the faith.
   b) 6–16. He raises humanity above angelhood.
   c) 17–18. Through his high priesthood.
3. His superiority over Moses.
   a) 1–6. Exalted above Moses.
   b) 7–19. Warnings from the fathers.
4. Christ not Moses leads to rest.
   a) 1–13. There is a rest remaining.
   b) 14–16. Hold fast the confession.
   Part II. The high priesthood of Christ, 5–7.
5. After the type of Melchizedek.
   a) 1–10. Priest after order of Melchizedek.
   b) 11–14. Ignorance of this typical relation.
6. Exhortation to press on unto perfection.
   a) 1–8. The exhortation to press on.
   b) 9–20. Encouraged by sure hope in Christ.

7. The superiority of Melchizedek's priesthood.
   a) 1-10. Threefold superiority over Levitical priests.
   b) 11-28. Christ's office likewise eternal.
   PART III. Christ's new and better Covenant, 9-10.
8. Christ the minister of this Covenant.
   a) 1-5. His seat at the right hand of God.
   b) 6-13. The better promises of the new Covenant.
9. Christ the fulfilment of O. T. types.
   a) 1-10. Mosaic sanctuary points to Christ.
   b) 11-22. Approach to God through Christ's blood.
   c) 23-28. Necessary but unrepeated death of Christ.
10. Recapitulations and warnings.
    a) 1-18. Recapitulations and summary.
    b) 19-25. Exhortation: be faithful to Christ.
    c) 26-39. The reward of faithfulness.
    PART IV. Consequent practical lessons, 11-13.
11. Lesson from the heroes of faith.
    a) 1-7. Patterns of faith before Abraham.
    b) 8-19. Example of Abraham and Sarah.
    c) 20-29. Examples from Isaac to Moses.
    d) 30-40. Later Old Testament examples.
12. Appeal to endure God's chastening.
    a) 1 13. Encouragements from those witnesses.
    b) Exhortation to unity and holiness.
    c) 18-29. The greater guilt of apostacy from Christ.
13. Conclusion of the Epistle.
    a 1-6. General practical exhortation.
    b) 7-17. Special warning against apostacy.
    c) 18-25. Personal communications.

A.D. 45. 25. PAULINE PERIOD. GENTILE CHRISTIANITY. Acts 13-28.
Hurlbut, pages 116-131.

§ 1. FIRST MISSIONARY JOURNEY. Acts 13-14.

Acts. 13. Journey from Antioch to Iconium.
   a) 1-3. Paul and Barnabas chosen to be missionaries.
   b) 4-12. Result of their labor in Cyprus.
   c) 13-41. Arrival at and Paul's address in Antioch (of Pisidia).
   d) 42-52. Expelled from the city by the Jews.
14. Journey to Lystra and back to Antioch in Syria.
   a) 1-7. Success and disturbance in Iconium.
   b) 8-20. The attempt at Lystra to worship them.
   c) 21-28. Return journey confirming believers.

§ 2. SECOND MISSIONARY JOURNEY, 15-18: 22.

15. Apostolic council and start on second journey.
   a) 1-5. Difficulty between Jewish and Gentile Christians.
   b) 6-21. Course of proceedings at the Council.
   c) 22-35. The settlement by compromise.
   d) 36-41. The start on the second journey.
16. Paul and Silas imprisoned in Philippi.
   a) 1-10. Journey through Asia and call to Macedonia.
   b) 11-18. Success and disturbance at Philippi.
   c) 19-34. Conversion of Philippian jailor.
   d) 35-40. Secret release of Paul and Silas.

17. Work in Thessalonica, Boerea and Athens.
    a) 1-9. Labors and experience in Thessalonica.
    b) 10-15. The nobility of the Boereans.
    c) 16-21. Paul's observations in Athens.
    d) 22-34. Paul's address to the Athenians.
18 : 1-22. Paul at Corinth. Close of second journey.
    a) 1-17. Paul's labors and result at Corinth.
    b) 18-22. His return home.
  §3. FIRST GROUP OF EPISTLES. ON ESCHATOLOGY.

I THESSALONIANS. CONSOLATION FROM SECOND ADVENT.

    PART I. Review of Paul's relation to them, 1-3.
1. Thanksgiving for their state of grace, 2-10.
2. Personal appeal to his readers.
    a) 1-12. Appeal to them as to his ministry.
    b) 13-16. Their steadfastness.
    c) 17-20. His desire to visit them.
3. What he had done for them.
    a) 1-5. He had sent Timothy to them.
    b) 6-13. His prayer in their behalf.
    PART II. Exhortation and consolation, 4-5.
4. Purity, diligence and comfort.
    a) 1-12. Be pure and diligent.
    b) 13-18. Comfort concerning their dead.
5. The coming of the Lord.
    a) 1-11. Be watchful and sober, for he comes unexpected.
    b) 12-24. Closing exhortations.
    c) 25-28. Salutation and benediction.

II THESSALONIANS. AWAIT PATIENTLY THE DAY OF THE LORD.

1. Consolation under fresh persecution, 1-12.
2. The doctrine of the man of sin. Exhortations.
    a) 1-12. The doctrine of the man of sin.
    b) 13-17. Exhortation to steadfastness.
3. Conclusion.
    a) 1-15. Closing exhortation
    b) 16-18. Salutation and benediction.

  §4. THIRD MISSIONARY JOURNEY, Acts 18 : 22-21 : 16.
Acts. 18 : 23-28. Paul's visits and Apollos' labors.
19. Paul at Ephesus.
    a) 1-7. Paul and the disciples of John.
    b) 8-12. Paul's work in Ephesus.
    c) 13-20. Suppression of witchcraft.
    d) 21-41. Tumult in Ephesus.
    (I Corinthians written.)
20. Through Macedonia and Greece back to Miletus.
    a) 1-6. Through Macedonia and Greece back to Troas.
    (II Cor., Galatians, Romans.)
    b) 7-16. Miracle at Troas and return to Miletus.
    c) 17-38. Paul's farewell to Ephesian elders.
21 : 16. Conclusion of the journey.
    a) 1-7. The journey to Caesarea.
    b) 8-16. Journey to Jerusalem.
  §5. SECOND GROUP OF EPISTLES. ON JUDAIC CONTROVERSY·

I CORINTHIANS. ON MORALITY AND DISCIPLINE.

PART I. The sin of party spirit, 1-4.
1. Exhortation to unity. His self-defense.
   a) 1-9. Address and introduction.
   b) 10-17. Exhortation to unity.
   c) 18-31. Defense of his method of preaching.
2. The Gospel has its own wisdom.
   a) 1-5. His own humility.
   b) 6-16. The Gospel's wisdom revealed to Christians.
3. Rebuke of their contentions and schisms.
   a) 1-4. Justification of his method of teaching.
   b) 5-15. Relation of teachers to their Master and work.
   c) 16-23. Rebuke of their conceit as cause of schisms.
4. Correction of their party errors.
   a) 1-5. How to judge a minister.
   b) 6-13. Reproof of their party pride.
   c) 14-21. Paternal address and warning.

PART II. Disorders in their church, 5-6.
5. The incestuous offenders.
   a) 1-8. Accusation and reproof.
   b) 9-13. Correction of a misunderstanding.
6. Be separate from the world.
   a) 1-11. Litigations with unbelievers.
   b) 12-20. Avoid impurity.

PART III. Answers to their questions, 7-16.
7. Concerning marriage and celibacy.
   a) 1-17. Marriage and its duties.
   b) 18-24. The believer and his circumstances.
   c) 25-40. Concerning celibacy.
8. Things sacrificed and Christian freedom, 1-13.
9. Paul's renunciation of his rights.
   a) 1-18. Statement of his rights as apostle.
   b) 19-23. Accommodating himself to surroundings.
   c) 24-27. Striving for the crown.
10. Warnings against abuse of Christian freedom.
    a) 1-13. Examples from the fathers.
    b) 14-22. Flee from idolatry.
    c) 23-11:1. Rule for questions of conscience.
11. Head-dress in church. Lord's supper.
    a) 2-16. Women's heads covered, men's not.
    b) 17-34. Agape and Lord's supper.
12. The manifold gifts of the spirit.
    a) 1-10. Many gifts for the church's welfare.
    b) 11-20. The unity of the giving spirit.
    c) 21-31. The equality of the members.
13. Supremacy of love above gifts.
    a) 1-3. Gifts without love worthless.
    b) 4-7. Nature of love.
    c) 8-13. Eternity of love.
14. Prophecy and speaking with tongues.
    a) 1-25. Supremacy of prophecy over tongues.
    b) 26-40. Rules their right use.

15. Defense of doctrine resurrection.
    - a) 1–11. The fact of Christ's resurrection.
    - b) 12–34. The proof of the resurrection.
    - c) 35–54. The how of the resurrection.
    - d) 55–58. Triumph and encouragement.
16. Collection. His helpers. Conclusion.
    - a) 1–9. Concerning the collection.
    - b) 10–18. Treatment of his friends.
    - c) 19–24. Salutation and autograph.

II CORINTHIANS. PAUL'S DEFENSE OF HIS APOSTLESHIP.

PART I. His apostolic character and conduct, 1–7.

1. Introduction and self-justification.
    - a) 1–11. Greeting and affectionate introduction.
    - b) 12–24. Justification of his conduct.
2. Paul's thoughtfulness of his converts.
    - a) 1–11. Needless sorrow to be spared.
    - b) 12–17. Paul's concern for the Corinthian.
3. Glorification of the Christian ministry.
    - a) 1–11. Praise of his ministry is not self praise.
    - b) 12–18. Results of the old and the new ministry.
4. Paul's life as a minister.
    - a) 1–6. His faithfulness in the ministry.
    - b) 7–18. Personal suffering and glory of his office.
5. Continued explanation of his conduct.
    - a) 1–10. Continuation of 4:7–18.
    - b) 11–21. His is a ministry of reconciliation.
6. His ministry of edification.
    - a) 1–10. Also of edification by blameless life.
    - b) 11–7:1. Earnest appeal for purity of life.
7. 2–16. Impression and result of his first letter.

PART II. Contributions for the poor, 8–9.

8. Praise of liberality. Titus the collector.
    - a) 1–15. Their liberality praised and encouraged.
    - b) 16–24. Commendation of Titus and his helpers.
9. Admonition and reward.
    - a) 1–5. Admonition to give speedily.
    - b) 6–15. The blessing of a cheerful giver.

PART III. Direct personal self defence, 10–13.

10. His *works* praise him.
    - a) 1–9. Appeal to his success.
    - b) 10–18. Not *he* needs self commendation.
11. Paul's boasting in contrast to his opponents.
    - a) 1–15 He served gratuitously.
    - b) 16–33. He is all and more than his opponents.
12. Continuation of chapter 11.
    - a) 1–6. His revelation as ground for boasting.
    - b) 7–10. He is kept humble by thorn in the flesh.
    - c) 11–18. Corinthians blamed for his boasting.
13. His desire to avoid disciplining them.
    - a) 12:19–21. Correction of some faults.
    - b) 13:1–10. Admonition to spare him discipline.
    - c) 11–14. Encouragement and benediction.

GALATIANS. CHRISTIAN LIBERTY.

PART I. Personal. Vindication of apostleship, 1–2.

1. Introduction and first argument.
   a) 1–10. Greeting and occasion of the epistle.
   b) 11–24. His gospel from God, not man.
2. His equality with other apostles shown.
   a) 1–10. Because they acknowledged his equal mission.
   b) 11–22. In his correction of Peter.

PART II. Doctrinal. Freedom from the law, 3–4.

3. Salvation by faith alone.
   a) 1–5. Proved by their own experience.
   b) 6–18. Taught by the Old Testament.
   c) 19–29. The law was only to lead to Christ.
4. The Christian's freedom from the law.
   a) 1–7. Under the law is a state of minority.
   b) 8–11. Their inclination to return to tutelage.
   c) 12–20. Affectionate personal appeal.
   d) 21–31. The allegory of Sarah and Hagar.

PART III. Practical. Exhortation, 5–6.

5. Nature and use of Christian liberty.
   a) 1–12. Nature of Christian freedom.
   b) 13–26. Exhortation to right use of liberty.
6. Concluding exhortations.
   a) 1–10. Exhortation to various duties of love.
   b) 11–18. Summary review. Benediction.

ROMANS. SALVATION BY FAITH, 1: 16, 17.

PART I. Christ our righteousness, 1–5.

1. Salutation. Introduction. Heathen depravity.
   a) 1–7. Salutation.
   b) 8–17. Introduction, thanks and theme.
   §1. Universal need of justification, 1: 18–5: 20.
   c) 18–32. The fallen state of the Gentiles.
2. The Jews' need of justification through Christ.
   a) 1–11. They also are under divine wrath.
   b) 12–24. Having the law is of no avail.
   c) 25–29. Circumcision is of no avail.
3. Jewish advantages, sin, salvation by faith.
   a) 1–8. The value of Jewish privileges.
   b) 9–20. Universal sinfulness of man.
   §2. How full salvation is attained, 3: 21–5.
   c) 21–31. Proof of salvation by faith.
4. How salvation was attained in the Old Testament.
   a) 1–8. Abraham justified through faith.
   b) 9–17. Abraham as father of the faithful.
   c) 18–25. His faith and example.
5. How justification leads to full salvation.
   a) 1–11. The certainty of salvation to the believer.
   b) 12–21. Ruined in Adam, saved in Christ.

PART II. Christ our sanctification, 6–8.

6. Freedom from dominion of sin.
   a) 1–11. United with Christ and dead to sin.
   b) 12–23. True service and true freedom.

7. The law of the spirit and the law of the flesh.
    a) 1-6. The believer freed from the law.
    b) 7-13. The law provoking to sin.
    c) 14-25. Because of the power of sin in the flesh.
8. The believer's life in Christ.
    a) 1-11. The spirit is principle of the new life.
    b) 12-27. The spirit is the source of assurance.
    c) 28-29. The firmest ground of Christian assurance.

PART III. Temporary rejection of the Jews, 9-11.

9. Solution of the problem of the rejection.
    a) 1-5. Paul's love for Israel.
    b) 6-21. Freedom of God's choice of the fathers.
    c) 22-29. Justice of God's call of the Gentiles.
10. Rejected because they rejected God's salvation.
    a) 9:30-10:3. Jews to blame for their rejection.
    b) 4-13. The salvation they rejected.
    c) 14-21. Israel inexcusable.
11. God's final purpose with Israel.
    a) 1-10. Hardening of part of Israel.
    b) 11-24. Their rejection is a blessing to Gentiles.
    c) 25-26. Their salvation according to promise.

PART IV. Exhortation and instruction, 12-16.

12. The value of humility and love.
    a) 1-8. Exhortation to be humble.
    b) 9-21. To love the brethren.
13. Civil duties.
    a) 1-10. Duty of believers in civil relations.
    b) 11-14. Consecration.
14. Matters not binding on conscience.
    a) 1-12. Duty to the over-scrupulous.
    b) 13-23. On charitable judgment.
15. On tolerance. Conclusion of discussion.
    a) 1-13. Exhortation to Christian tolerance.
    b) 14-23. Conclusion of the discussion.
16. Commendation and salutation.
    a) 1-2. Commendation of Phœbe.
    b) 3-16. Apostle's salutation.
    c) 17-27. Warnings and salutations.

§6. PAUL'S IMPRISONMENT. Acts 21: 17-28.

Acts. 21: 17-40. Consultation and arrest.
    a) 17-26. Paul's consultation with James and the elders.
    b) 27-40. His arrest in Jerusalem.
  22. Paul's address to the people.
    a) 1-21. Paul's address in his defence.
    b) 22-30. Result of the address.
  23. Paul's trial and removal to Caesarea.
    a) 1-11. Paul before the Sanhedrim.
    b) 12-21. The occasion for his removal.
    c) 22-35. Paul removed to Caesarea.
  24. Paul before Felix.
    a) 1-9. Paul accused by Tertullus.
    b) 10-21. Paul's defence before Felix.
    c) 22-27. Paul's further treatment under Felix.

25. Paul brought before Festus.
   a) 1–5. Zeal of the Jews against Paul.
   b) 6–12. Trial before Festus and appeal to Caesar.
   c) 13–22. Consultation between Festus and Agrippa.
   d) 23–27. Paul brought before Festus and Agrippa.
26. Paul's apology before Agrippa and Festus.
   a) 1–23. The apology.
   b) 24–32. The impression it made.
27. On the journey to Rome as far as Melita.
   a) 1–13. From Caesarea to Crete.
   b) 14–26. The storm.
   c) 27–38. Approaching land.
   d) 39–44. Safely landed.
28. Arrival and stay at Rome.
   a) 1–10. Stay at Melita.
   b) 11–16. Journey to Rome.
   c) 17–28. Paul's intercourse with the Jews.

§ 7. THIRD GROUP OF EPISTLES. PERSONAL AND CHRISTOLOGICAL.
PHILIPPIANS. PAUL'S LOVE TO THE PHILIPPIANS.
1. Paul's joy in his Philippian converts.
   a) 1–11. Greeting, thanksgiving and prayer.
   b) 12–26. Paul's labors and success at Rome.
   c) 27–33. He urges them to live right.
2. Entreaty to follow Christ. Paul's helpers.
   a) 1–11. Entreaty to be Christlike.
   b) 12–18. God's help in following Christ.
   c) 19–30. Paul's helpers and co-laborers.
3. Warning against false Judaizing teachers.
   a) 1–16. Their spirit as distinguished from his.
   b) 17–4:1. Opposite destiny of false and true teachers.
4. Concluding admonition and thanks.
   a) 2–9. Exhortations.
   b) 10–20. Thanks for their gifts of love.
   c) 21–23. Salutation and benediction.

COLOSSIANS. CHRIST IS ALL IN ALL.
1. The blessings of salvation in Christ.
   a) 1–12. Thanksgiving and prayer.
   b) 13–23. The blessing of salvation.
   c) 24–29. Paul's joy in tribulation.
2. Warning concerning false teachers.
   a) 1–15. Paul's anxiety for his converts.
   b) 16–23. Two special warnings.
3. Exhortations.
   a) 1–11. Exhortation to mortify the earthly members.
   b) 12–17. Put on Christian virtues.
   c) 18–4:1. Domestic duties.
4. Precepts and salutations.
   a) 1–7. Precept concerning prayer and infidels.
   b) 8–18. Conclusion.

PHILEMON. PAUL'S INTERPOSITION FOR A SLAVE.
   a) 1–3. The greeting.
   b) 4–7. Thanksgiving for Philemon's piety.
   c) 8–22. Interposition in behalf of Onesimus.
   d) 23–25. Salutation and blessing.

EPHESIANS.
PART I. Glory of the Church of Christ, 1-3.
1. Salvation and destiny of believers.
    a) 1-14. God praised for salvation through Christ.
    b) 15-23. The destiny of believers.
2. From death in sin to life in Christ.
    a) 1-10. Once dead but now alive by faith.
    b) 11-22. Their better present condition.
3. Paul's office as apostle to the Gentiles.
    a) 1-13. The nature of his mission to the Gentiles.
    b) 14-21. His petition for them.

PART II. Walk worthy of your calling, 4-6.
4. Christian unity and conquest of sin.
    a) 1-16. Exhortation to Christian unity.
    b) 17-24. Perform the duties of the new life.
    c) 25-32. Exhortation to particular virtues.
5. Rules for the new life.
    a) 1-14. New life in divine fellowship and purity.
    b) 15-21. Be considerate.
    c) 22-33. Relation between wives and husbands.
6. Various exhortations.
    a) 1-9. Domestic duties.
    b) 10-20. Concluding exhortations.
    c) 21-24. Blessing.

§8. FOURTH GROUP. PASTORAL EPISTLES.

I TIMOTHY. PAUL'S CHARGE TO TIMOTHY.
1. Charge concerning doctrine.
    a) 1-11. Heresies.
    b) 12-20. Hold what I have taught you.
2. Concerning praying.
    a) 1-7. Pray for all men.
    b) 8-15. By whom and how.
3. Official ministry.
    a) 1-7. Dignity and nature of the bishop's office.
    b) 8-13. Character of deacons and deaconesses.
    c) 14-16. Importance of these admonitions.
4. Be vigilant.
    a) 1-5. Warnings against errorists.
    b) 6-16. Steadfastness and growth in his calling.

5 and 6. Management of the community.
    a) 5: 1-16. His conduct toward his flock.
    b) 5: 17-25. Concerning the elders.
    c) 6: 1-10. Slaves and false teachers.
    d) 6: 11-21. Address to Timothy. Conclusion.

TITUS. PAUL'S INSTRUCTION TO TITUS.
1. Directions for election of a bishop
    a) 1-4. Greeting.
    b) 5-9. Qualifications of a bishop.
    c) 10-16. Circumstances in Crete.
2. Direction for church members.
    a) 1-10. Their directions.
    b) 11-15. Their enforcement.

3. Directions to Titus.
    a) 1–11. Admonition of believers.
    b) 12–15. Final directions and greetings.

II TIMOTHY. PAUL'S LAST LETTER.

1. Stir up the gift within thee.
    a) 1–5. Introduction.
    b) 6–18. Admonition to stir up his gift.
2. Exhortation and precepts.
    a) 1–13. Exhortation to steadfastness.
    b) 14–26. Rules for pastoral conduct.
3. Future troublous times.
    a) 1–9. Warnings against false teachers.
    b) 10–17. Praise and admonition.
4. Paul's parting words.
    a) 1–7. Parting charge to Timothy.
    b) 8–18. Paul's loneliness and desertion.
    c) 19–22. Salutations.

26. JOHANNEAN PERIOD. SPIRITUAL CHRISTIANITY.
GOSPEL OF JOHN. BELIEVE IN CHRIST AND LIVE.

PART I. Development of faith in Christ, 1–4.

1. Prologue and testimonies to Christ.
    a) 1–18. Prologue. The Word, Faith, Unbelief.
    b) 19–37. John's testimony.
    c) 38–52. The awakening of faith.
2. Testimony of his works.
    a) 1–12. Faith confirmed by a miracle.
    b) 13–22. Faith confirmed by prophecy.
    c) 23–25. Outbursts of faith through signs.
3. New and eternal life by faith in Christ.
    a) 1–10. The question of the new birth.
    b) 11–21. Faith the condition of regeneration.
    c) 22–36. John's further testimony to Christ.
4. Samaritan and Galilean faith in Christ.
    a) 1–26. Samaritan woman's faith in Christ.
    b) 27–38. Christ's delight in saving souls.
    c) 39–42. The Samaritan's faith in Christ.
    d) 43–54. The faith of the Galileans.

PART II. Development of unbelief in Israel, 5–12.

5. First outburst of hatred in Judea.
    a) 1–18. The miracle and Sabbath controversy.
    b) 19–30. He is justified, for he works for the father.
    c) 31–47. The Father's corroboration of his testimony.
6. The great messianic testimony and sifting.
    a) 1–13. The miraculous feeding.
    b) 14–21. Jesus walks upon the water.
    c) 22–59. Jesus the bread of life.
    d) 60–71. The sifting of his followers.
7. The conflict. Attempt to arrest him.
    a) 1–13. Unbelief of his brethren.
    b) 14–36. Self-defence. His teaching, origin and end.
    c) 37–52. Failure of the attempted arrest.

8. The conflict. Their contradictions.
    a) 7: 53–8: 11. The adulteress forgiven.
    b) 12–20. Pharisees oppose the light of the world.
    c) 21–29. I am he.
    d) 30–59. Contrast between himself and the Jews.
9. The Jews persecute the healed blind man.
    a) 1–12. Healing of the man born blind.
    b) 13–34. The healed one under inquisition.
    c) 35–41. Jesus confirms his faith.
10. Rejection of the true shepherd.
    a) 1–21. Jesus the true shepherd.
    b) 22–31. Attempt to stone Jesus.
    c) 32–42. Accusation of blasphemy.
11. Jesus the resurrection and the life.
    a) 1–16. Death of Lazarus.
    b) 17–33. Martha and Mary's faith in Jesus.
    c) 34–44. Raising of Lazarus.
    d) 45–57. The council to kill him.
12. Christ's final self-revelation to Israel.
    a) 1–11. The anointing at Bethany.
    b) 12–19. Triumphant entry into Jerusalem.
    c) 20–36. His last appearance in the temple.

PART III. Development of faith in his disciples, 13–21.

13. Purifying the apostles.
    a) 1–20. The lesson of humility.
    b) 21–30. The removal of Judas.
    c) 31–36. The betrayal foretold.
14. The great address of comfort.
    a) 1–11. Prediction of his second coming.
    b) 12–24. Comforting assurances.
    c) 25–31. The comforter promised.
15. New relations of the believers.
    a) 1–17. The believer's relation to Christ.
    b) 18–16: 4. Consequent opposition of the world.
16. Victory and joy of his followers.
    a) 5–15. Victory through the spirit.
    b) 16–33. His parting words.
17. The great High Priestly prayer.
    a) 1–5. The prayer to be glorified.
    b) 6–19. Intercession for his disciples.
    c) 20–26. Intercession for all believers.
18. Jesus on trial before unbelievers.
    a) 1–11. The arrest.
    b) 12–27. Peter's denial.
    c) 28–40. Trial before Pilate.
19. Unbelief and Jesus triumphant.
    a) 1–12. Apparent success of unbelief.
    b) 13–22. Jesus' glorious humiliation.
    c) 23–40. His triumph *in* death.
20. The disciples' faith in him justified.
    a) 1–10. Proof of his resurrection to Peter and John.
    b) 11–18. Proof to Mary Magdalene.
    c) 19–31. Proof to the other disciples.
21. Christ's appearance at the sea of Galilee.
    a) 1–14. Christ appears to them at the sea of Galilee.
    b) 15–25. Reinstatement of Peter.

I JOHN. JOY IN THE CERTAINTY OF LIFE IN CHRIST.
1. Evidence from walking in the light.
     a) 1-4. Introduction.
     b) 5-2:2. Freedom from sin.
2. Walking in the light shown by
     a) 3-13. Brotherly love.
     b) 14-27. Separation from the world.
3. The evidence of divine sonship shown by
     a) 1-10. Righteous conduct toward God.
     b) 11-18. Righteous conduct toward man.
     c) 19-23. Recapitulation.
4. The source of sonship is in the spirit.
     a) 1-6. It teaches to confess Christ.
     b) 7-12. To love one another.
     c) 13-28. Recapitulation.
5. Eternal life through faith.
     a) 1-12. The power of faith.
     b) 13-21. The conclusion.

II JOHN. WARNINGS AGAINST ANTICHRIST, vss. 1-13.

III JOHN. EXHORTATION TO STEADFASTNESS, vss. 1-14.

THE REVELATION. THE FUTURE OF CHRIST'S KINGDOM.

PART I. Letters to the seven churches, 1-3.
1. Introduction and first vision.
     a) 1-8. Title, dedication and theme.
     b) 9-20. John's first vision of Christ.
2. Letters to Ephesus, Smyrna, Pergamos and Thyatira.
     a) 1-7. To the mother church at Ephesus.
     b) 8-11. To the martyr church at Smyrna.
     c) 12-17. To the martyr church at Pergamos.
     d) 18-29. To the idolatrous church at Thyatira.
3. Letters to Sardis, Philadelphia and Laodicea.
     a) 1-6. To the spiritually half-dead church at Sardis.
     b) 7-13. To the tried church at Philadelphia.
     c) 14-22. To the lukewarm church at Laodicea.

PART II. The seven seals, 4-7.
4. Vision of the enthroned God, 1-11.
5. The sealed book of the world's history.
     a) 1-5. The sealed book.
     b) 6-14. The Lamb worthy to open it.
6. Opening the first six seals.
     a) 1-8. The white, red, black and pale horses.
     b) 9-17. Souls under the altar. Earthquake.
7. The sealing of the believers.
     a) 1-8. The sealing.
     b) 9-17. The saints adoring God.

PART III. The seven trumpets, 8-11.
8. The seventh seal and first four trumpets.
     a) 1-6. The angels with the trumpets.
     b) 7-13. The blowing of the first four trumpets.
9. The blowing of the fifth and sixth trumpets.
     a) 1-12. The fifth trumpet and first woe.
     b) 13-21. The sixth trumpet and second woe.

10. The seven thunders concerning the end, 1–11.
11. The testimony and seventh trumpet.
    a) 1–14. The testimony of the faithful.
    b) 15–19. Seventh trumpet and third woe.
        PART IV. The seven mystic figures, 12–14.
12. The sun-clad woman, red dragon and man-child.
    a) 1–6. These three mystic beings.
    b) 7–17. Satan cast down to earth.
13. The beasts from sea and land.
    a) 1–10. The wild sea-beast.
    b) 11–18. The wild land-beast.
14. The Lamb. The Son of Man.
    a) 1–13. The Lamb on Mt. Zion.
    b) 14–20. The Son of Man on the cloud.
        PART V. The seven bowls, 15–16.
15. Preparation for the seven bowls.
    a) 1–4. Song of Moses and of the Lamb.
    b) 5–8. The seven plagues in the bowls.
16. The outpouring of the six bowls, 1–21.
        PART VI. Doom of the foes of Christ, 17–20.
17. Vision of Babylon.
    a) 1–6. The vision of the mysterious woman.
    b) 7–18. Explanation of the vision.
18. Babylon is fallen.
    a) 1–20. Worldmen lament.
    b) 21–24. Christians rejoice.
19. The beast.
    a) 1–10. The harlot and the bride.
    b) 11–16. Preparation for the battle with beast.
    c) 17–21. Judgment on the beast.
20. Satan's last effort.
    a) 1–5. Millennial reign.
    b) 6–10. Satan's wars.
    c) 11–15. The book of life opened.
        PART VII. The blessed consummation, 21–22.
21. The renewal of heaven and earth.
    a) 1–8. The New Heaven and New Earth.
    b) 9–21. The heavenly Jerusalem.
    c) 22–22:5. The city of God. Gentile believers.
22:6–21. Epilogue.
    a) 6–11. The angel and John.
    b) 12–17. Jesus author of Revelations.
    c) 18–21. The sacredness of Revelations.

LIST OF HELPS TO BIBLE STUDY.

On the Whole Bible.

Speaker's Commentary.
Fraser, Synoptical Lectures.
Hurlbut, Manual of Biblical Geography.
Thomson, Land and the Book.
Tristram, Land of Israel.
―――― Sinai and Palestine.
―――― Fauna and Flora of Palestine.
Stanley, Sinai and Palestine.
Harris, Natural History of Palestine.
Graser, W. H., Trees and Plants of Palestine.
Hart, H. C., Animals of the Bible.
Bissel, Biblical Antiquities.
Keil, Biblical Archæology.
Briggs, Biblical Study.
Barrows, Sacred Geography and Antiquities.
Smith, Dictionary of the Bible.
Schaff, Dictionary of the Bible.
Kitto, Encyclopedia of Biblical Literature.

Contemporary History.

Rawlinson, The Seven Great Monarchies.
―――― History of Ancient Egypt.
Ancient History from the Monuments.
Wilkinson, Manners and Customs of Ancient Egyptians.
Schrader, Cuneiform Inscriptions and the Old Testament.
Records of the Past, Second Series.
Prideaux, Old and New Testaments Connected.
Curtis, The History of Greece.
Momsen, The History of Rome.

Old Testament.

Kurtz, History of the Old Testament Covenant.
Geikie, Hours with the Bible.
Smith, Old Testament History.
Stanley, History of the Jewish Church.
Josephus' Works.
Milman's History of the Jews.
Edersheim, Bible History.
Geikie, Old Testament Characters.
Orelli, Old Testament Prophecy.
Briggs, Messianic Prophecy.
Delitsch, Messianic Prophecy.
Oehler, Old Testament Theology.
Rawlinson, The Religions of the Ancient World.

PENTATEUCH.

Bissel, The Pentateuch.
Green, Moses and the Prophets.
Hengstenberg, The Books of Moses and Egypt.

GENESIS.

Lenormant, Beginnings of History.
Dodds, Bible Hand Book on Genesis.
Smith, Chaldean Genesis.
Ebers, Egypt and the Books of Moses.

PERIOD OF ADAM.

Geikie, Vol. 1, Chaps. 1-11.
Proper names in Dictionaries and Encyclopedias.
Sin, creation, serpent in Dictionary.

PERIOD OF NOAH.

Geikie, Vol. 1, Chaps. 12-17.
Schrader, in loco.

PERIOD OF ABRAHAM.

Geikie, Vol. 1, Chaps. 18-22.
Stanley, Lectures 1 and 2.
Tomkins, Times of Abraham, Men of the Bible.
Proper names, etc., in Dictionaries and Encyclopedias.

PERIOD OF ISAAC AND JACOB.

Geikie, Vol. 1, Chap. 23.
Stanley, Lectures 2 and 3.
Rawlinson, Isaac and Jacob, Men of the Bible.

PERIOD OF JOSEPH.

Geikie, Vol. 1, Chap. 24.
Stanley, Lecture 4.
Taylor, W. M., Joseph the Prime Minister.

JOB.

Cambridge Bible, Job.
Green, W. H., The Argument of the Book of Job.

PERIOD OF MOSES.

Geikie, Vol. 2, Chaps. 1-12.
Stanley, Lectures 5-9.
Rawlinson, Moses, His Life and Times, Men of the Bible.
Taylor, W. M., Moses the Lawgiver.
Ebers, Uaida, Joshua.
Laws of Moses, Tabernacle in Smith's Dictionary.
Bissel, Antiquities, Chaps. 11-14.
Ebers, Durch Gosen zum Sinai.
Proper names and topics in Dictionaries and Encyclopedias.

PERIOD OF JOSHUA.

Geikie, Vol. 2, Chap. 13.
Stanley, Lectures 10-12.
Deane, W. J., Joshua, His Life and Times, Men of Bible.
Cambridge Bible, Joshua.
Douglas, The Gospel in the Book of Joshua.

Period of the Judges.
Geikie, Vol. 2, Chaps. 14–16.
Stanley, Lectures 13–16.
Cambridge Bible, Judges.
Dodds, Israel's Iron Age.
Douglas, Joshua and Judges, T. & T. Clark.

Period of Samuel.
Geikie, Vol. 3, Chaps. 1–3.
Stanley, Lectures 17–20.
Samuel and Saul, Men of the Bible.
Cambridge Bible, I and II Samuel.
Murphy, Chronicles, T. & T. Clark.

Period of Saul.
Geikie, Vol. 3, Chaps. 4–5.
Stanley, Vol. 2, Lecture 21.
Magic in Smith's Dictionary.

Period of David.
Geikie, Vol. 3, Chaps. 6–13.
Stanley, Lectures 22–25.
David, Men of the Bible.
Taylor, W. M., David King of Israel.
Maclaren, Life of David as Reflected in the Psalms.
Cambridge Bible, Psalms.
Murphy, Psalms, T. & T. Clark.

Period of Solomon.
Geikie, Vol. 3, Chaps. 14–18.
Stanley, Lectures 26–28.
Griffis, The Lily Among Thorns.
Solomon, Men of the Bible.
Delitsch, Song of Solomon.
Temple in Smith's Dictionary.
Cambridge Bible, 1 and 2 Kings, Ecclesiastes.

Period of the Division.
Geikie, Vol. 4, Chaps. 1–5.
Stanley, Lectures 29–31, 35–36.
Rawlinson, Kings of Judah and Israel.
Taylor, Life of Elijah.

Syrian Period.
Geikie, Vol. 4, Chap. 6.
Stanley, Lectures 32–33.

Period of the Restoration.
Geikie, Vol. 4, Chap. 7.
Stanley, Lecture 37.

Period of the Fall of Israel.
Geikie, Vol. 4, Chaps. 8–11.
Stanley, Lectures 34 and 37.
Farrar, The Minor Prophets, Men of the Bible.
Cambridge Bible, Hosea, Obadiah and Jonah.
Orelli, Commentary on Isaiah and Jeremiah.
Barnes, Notes on Isaiah.
Delitsch, Isaiah.
Driver, Isaiah, Men of the Bible.
Klosterman, Isaiah in Hertzog Encyclopedia, 2d edition.

Period of Hezekiah.

Geikie, Vol. 4, Chaps. 12-17.
Stanley, Lecture 28.
Farrar, Minor Prophets, Micah, Nahum.
Cambridge Bible, Micah.

Period of Decline and Fall of Jerusalem.

Geikie, Vol. 5, Chaps. 2-18, Vol. 6, 1-8.
Stanley, Lectures 39 and 40.
Cambridge Bible, Jeremiah.
Cheyne, Jeremiah, Men of the Bible.

Apocrypha, etc.

Bissel, Apocrypha.
Beecher, J. W., Post Exilian History of Israel, Old Testament Student, Vols. 9 and 10.
Drummond, Jas., The Jewish Messiah.
Skinner, John, Historical Connection, T. & T. Clark.
Redford, Four Centuries of Silence.

Period of the Captivity.

Geikie, Vol. 5, Chap. 19, Vol. 6, Chaps. 9-16.
Stanley, Lectures 40 end, 41, 42.
Cambridge Bible, Ezekiel.
Deane, H., Daniel, Men of the Bible.

Persian Period.

Geikie, Vol. 6, Chaps. 17-21.
Stanley, Lectures 43-45.
Cambridge Bible, Haggai, Zechariah and Malachi.
The same in Bible Hand Book, T. & T. Clark.
Ebers, An Egyptian Princess.
Proper name in Dictionaries and Encyclopedias.

Grecian Period.

Stanley, Lectures 46-47.
Curtius, History of Greece during this period.

Period of Independence.

Stanley, Lectures 48-49.
Longfellow, Judas Maccabeus.

Roman Period.

Stanley, Lecture 50.
Momsen, Roman History during this time.

On the New Testament.

Farrar, Messages of the Books.
Lumby, Introduction to New Testament.
Dodds, Introduction to New Testament.
Smith, New Testament History.
Meyer's Commentary.

Life of Christ.

Cambridge Bible on the Gospels.
Life of Christ, Stalker, Andrews, Farrar, Geikie.
Schürer, History of Jews in Time of Christ, American edition.
Stalker, Imago Christi.
Delitsch, Jewish Artizan Life in Time of Christ.
Wallace, Ben Hur.
Prince of the House of David.

Petrine Period.

Howson, Horæ Petrinæ.
Taylor, Peter the Apostle.
Lumby, Acts of the Apostles.
Cambridge Bible, Acts, Epistles of Peter, Jude, Hebrews.
Schaff, History of the Christian Church, Vol. I.

Pauline Period.

Conybeare & Howson, Life and Epistles of St. Paul.
Farrar, Life of Paul.
Stalker, Life of St. Paul.
Howson, The Companions of Paul.
Cambridge Bible, Acts, Romans, Galatians, Corinthians, Phil., Thess.
Sabatier, The Apostle Paul.
Stevens, G. B., The Pauline Theology.

Johannean Period.

Godet, The Gospel of John.
Cambridge Bible, John, Epistles of John, Revelation.
McDonald, Life and Writings of St. John.

DIRECTIONS FOR STUDYING THE BIBLE.

1. Study the "Synopsis" by Stages and Epochs, and commit it to memory.
2. Read a book of the Bible through, noting the synopsis of it as given in the fore part of the Outlines.
3. Read each chapter, noting the subdivisions as given in the Outlines and mark dark passages.
4. Read each subdivision of a chapter and see whether the headings are correct. Suggest your own division with heading.
5. State in detail to yourself, or some other person, what the chapter says.
6. Read the chapter again to correct and complete your statement of its contents.
7. Use the helps on dark passages and other material needing help.
8. At the end of a section or book give a connected statement of the idea in it.
9. Commit the synopsis of the book.

INDEX.

	Page.		Page.
Acts	11, 83.	Judith	9, 65.
Amos	8, 57.	Kings I	8, 46, 48.
Baruch	10, 78.	Kings II	8, 49, 54.
Bel and the Dragon	9, 62.	Lamentations	58.
Christ, Life of	80.	Leviticus	6, 23.
Chronicles I	7, 8, 37, 48.	Luke	10, 80.
Chronicles II	8, 46, 54.	Maccabees I	10, 75.
Colossians	12, 92.	Maccabees II	10, 77.
Corinthians I	11, 88.	Malachi	10.
Corinthians II	11, 89.	Manasses, Prayer of	
Daniel	9, 62.	Mark	10, 80.
Deuteronomy	6, 28.	Matthew	10, 80.
Ecclesiastes	8, 47.	Micah	8, 51.
Ecclesiasticus	10, 72.	Nahum	9, 53.
Ephesians	12, 93.	Nehemiah	10, 68.
Esdras I	10, 69.	Numbers	6, 25.
Esdras II	10, 70.	Obadiah	50.
Esther	10, 68.	Peter I	11, 85.
Exodus	6, 20.	Peter II	11, 85.
Ezekiel	9, 58.	Philemon	12, 92.
Ezra	9, 66.	Philippians	12, 92.
Galatians	11, 90.	Proverbs	7, 47.
Genesis	5, 13.	Psalms	7, 39.
Habakkuk	9, 55.	Revelation	12, 96.
Haggai	10, 67.	Romans	11, 90.
Hebrews	11, 85.	Ruth	7, 34.
Hosea	8, 51.	Samuel I	7, 35.
Isaiah, 1–39	8, 52.	Samuel II	7, 37.
Isaiah, 40–66	9, 63.	Song of Songs	7, 47.
James	11, 84.	Song of the Holy Children	62.
Jeremiah	9, 55.	Susanna	9, 61.
Job	6, 16.	Thessalonians I	11, 87.
Joel	8, 50.	Thessalonians II	11, 87.
John	10, 12, 94.	Timothy I	12, 93.
John I	12, 96.	Timothy II	12, 94.
John II	12, 96.	Titus	12, 93.
John III	12, 96.	Tobit	9, 64.
Jonah	8, 51.	Wisdom of Solomon	10, 78.
Joshua	6, 31.	Zechariah	10, 67.
Jude	11, 84.	Zephaniah	9, 55.
Judges	7, 33.		

www.ingramcontent.com/pod-product-compliance
Lightning Source LLC
Chambersburg PA
CBHW030409170426
43202CB00010B/1548